TIME IS UP
RAPTURED

Dr. Richard E. Weathers Psy. D.

Copyright © 2023 Dr. Richard E. Weathers Psy. D.

All rights reserved. No part of this book may be reproduced, stored, or transmitted by any means—whether auditory, graphic, mechanical, or electronic—without written permission of both publisher and author, except in the case of brief excerpts used in critical articles and reviews. Unauthorized reproduction of any part of this work is illegal and is punishable by law.

ISBN: 979-8-88640-767-9 (sc)
ISBN: 979-8-88640-768-6 (hc)
ISBN: 979-8-88640-769-3 (e)

Because of the dynamic nature of the Internet, any web addresses or links contained in this book may have changed since publication and may no longer be valid. The views expressed in this work are solely those of the author and do not necessarily reflect the views of the publisher, and the publisher hereby disclaims any responsibility for them.

One Galleria Blvd., Suite 1900, Metairie, LA 70001
1-888-421-2397

CONTENTS

Author's Bio v
Preface ix

PART I: TIME IS UP

Chapter 1   Raptured My Vision of the Catching—
Away of the Church 3
Chapter 2   God's Time Line for the Rapture 22
Chapter 3 39

PART II: RAPTURE

Chapter 4 60
Chapter 5   Review of All These Things 75

Conclusion 85
References 95
Index 97

AUTHOR'S BIO

Richard Weathers was born on August 21, 1949 in Sedalia, Missouri.

He went into service (navy) at the age of nineteen, May 4, 1969. Served during the Vietnam War. Honorable discharged on February 4, 1971.

He lived in Kansas City, Missouri, until 1975. Moved to Springfield, Missouri, and has lived there until present, 2013.

Attended
    Kingsway Christian College
    901 19th Street
    Des Moines, Iowa
    Theological Seminary
    Des Moines, Iowa

Master of Scriptural Psychology
    September 1997-October 1999
    Graduated with honors

Doctorate of Scriptural Psychology
    September 1999-May 24, 2000
    Graduated with honors

Started Ministry
    Born again at 7:30 p.m. on March 27, 1983

Started Serving
   March 28, 1983

Director of School of Ministry
Served September 1983 to May 1986
Cornerstone Church— Springfield, Missouri
Pastors—Jess and Paula Gibson

Prison Ministry (1984 to 1998)
Fordland Correctional Center
Fordland, Missouri (whole state of Missouri)

Pastor (1998 to 2002)
Spirit-Life Church
Springfield, Missouri

Evangelist from (2002 to 2013)
Springfield area

Now one of four senior pastors
Grace and Faith Fellowship
1950 W. South Glenstone
Springfield, Missouri

Thanks to all my Christian friends and family.

Especially my brother and sister in the Lord. Otis and Nell Villines—what strong friends they have been, and the strength they have given me throughout the years. Pastor Gerry and Rosie Bryant, who encouraged me when I was down in the ministry and helped me get up and keep going.

My sister Victoria who, throughout my life, was always there for me, building me up, always positive about us becoming someone someday. We finally arrived when we met the Lord as our Savior.

Thanks to my wife, Kay; without her I wouldn't be writing this today. She has stood by me for thirty-three years of our marriage and has partnered with me in the ministry, the one that has always made me a better man of God. My daughter, Tonyja, and her husband, Steve; and my son, Justin, and his wife, Heather; a daughter and a son who have made their father and mother proud of them. Four grandchildren—Tanner, Taylor, Hailey, and Haiden—the best grandchildren a proud grandfather could ever have.

My grandson Tanner is the one who helped me design the cover for this book.

There are many others—too numerous to name—but I want each of them to know how much they mean to me.

Thank you all for being such a valuable part of our lives.

PREFACE

All that you will read in the chapters of this book was given to me by the Lord. I have put it down just the way I believe God revealed it to me. If this book blesses you, it will be because of the Lord. I take no credit for revealing to you God's Word and revelation. Everything that I am or will ever be has been because of God's grace and love that he has poured into me. We are a product of his growth through his Holy Spirit. I am one of the least in his kingdom, but he has allowed me to share what he gave me forty years ago in 1973. May his words comfort you and set you free from the fear of this age.

Please take a few moments after reading this book and give the Lord a thank-you for this wonderful revelation of the catching-away of his church. Remember that he loves you with all his heart and that he is coming for you soon!

Dr. Richard E. Weathers, PsyD

PART I

TIME IS UP

CHAPTER 1

RAPTURED MY VISION OF THE CATCHING— AWAY OF THE CHURCH

Psalm 23
    To walk through the valley of the shadow of death, all we have to do is be born here on earth and grow up living in a world of sin, destruction, and darkness with death all around us.

Colossians 1:13
    Praise God that he loved us so much he decided not to leave us in this condition but has purchased for us a way out of this darkness and into the marvelous light of God's kingdom and his son's.

John 3:16
    This is not all there is to life but just the beginning of an exciting venture for all of us who obey God's plan of salvation (deliverance) through the precious blood of his son, Christ Jesus, who gave his life on the cross so we could live eternally.

Mark 10:27
Isaiah 7:14
    God knew that life could not come to us unless someone died—not just anyone but a sacrifice that would be sinless. With man, this would

be impossible, but with God, nothing is impossible, so he provided the perfect person for the job—his own son, Jesus, who willingly came down from heaven born of a virgin. He became a man, but without the sinful nature that we all inherit at birth, grew up not breaking the law (Ten Commandments), went to a cross of death that belonged to each of us, gave his physical life, shed his precious blood, and died in our place, giving us a legal right to enter into the kingdom of God through the cross of Calvary.

Luke 18:10

Because of Christ doing all the work and sacrifice of salvation to bring us back to his father, God, a lot of people will *not be* delivered or saved in this world because most of them want to be able to save themselves—usually through their good works or their religions—so their faith will not be in the work and person of Jesus Christ but in their own ability to attain righteousness in themselves (2 Tim. 3:5).

How sad that men have so much *pride* in themselves that they will miss the very thing they seek—eternal life with God.

But more on this later.

Right now I want to share with you a vision God gave to me in March of 1973.

A friend of mine and I were living in Blue Springs, Missouri, about thirty miles east of Kansas City, Missouri. I was working at the time for an insurance brokerage house, selling life-insurance policies to individuals, driving back and forth every day to work and home.

We lived in a little farmhouse three miles outside of town that had no well but a cistern. We had to order water by truck, and they delivered it. Water would flow through the pipe so we could wash dishes and take showers by gravity. Ray, my roommate, worked for the Blue Springs Police Department, so he was close to his workplace, and both of us were usually off work and home by 5:00 or 6:00 p.m. every night.

I was twenty-three years old at the time of this vision, and one month before God gave it to me, my earthly father had passed away with liver/colon cancer on February 4, 1973.

My heart was heavy with loss and the sorrow of not being able to see him again.

We were not as close as a son and father should have been, but I had always respected him as a dad who did his best to take care of thirteen children and a wife. We grew up poor in goods but always had the love of each other to make it through the hard times. All my brothers and sisters today still have a real close relationship with one another.

On the night God gave me the vision of the rapture of his church, it was late in the month of March—I believe it was the twenty-seventh. I'll explain why a little later in this book.

It was a normal day for me—got off work around 6:00 p.m., came home, ate dinner, watched TV, and went to bed around 10:00 p.m.

What was interesting about the vision was just before falling asleep, somewhere between closing my eyes and falling into a deep sleep, it was like all of a sudden I was taken out of my body—taken into the future where all colors and details were very clear.

But here I was, driving down a beautiful highway divided with hills that I thought were small mountains on both sides (up and down) with the clearest blue sky and green grass I had ever seen. It was like Technicolor—clear and beautiful. It was the most peaceful day that I had ever experienced. No bombs were falling, no plagues, war had not broken out in the USA—it was a peaceful day just like, I hope, today as you read these words to comfort you.

The Antichrist had not yet been loosed to control the world (Rev. 13:7-8, Rev. 6:1-2).

As I begin to drive up one of the hills, there was a valley in between the highway. Looking out of the windshield with both hands on the steering wheel, I began to see, developing in the clear blue sky, a small cloud the size of a hand that began to grow bigger and bigger. It started swirling like a scroll—like two ends of a sheet of paper that were rolled up together until they met in the middle.

Numbers 10:1

All of a sudden, the swirling stopped, and in the middle, it began to part and open up. The most beautiful sunlight that I had ever seen began to shine through. This sunlight was nothing Earth had ever seen before. It was like pure gold, translucent, and like the most radiant sunlight yet physical. As I kept looking out of my windshield, two angels appeared on both sides of this opening into heaven, dressed in white with two silver trumpets in their hands.

They put them to their lips, and the most wonderful sound that I had ever heard came forth. It sounded like running water/tinkling brass trumpets—*indescribable* (but one day, all who believe in Christ shall hear it). The instant I heard the sound, gravity turned loose of my body, and I began to rise up, out of my vehicle. The only way to describe the experience was that a greater power had taken control over natural earthly dominion. As I rose through the top of the roof of the car and as my eyes passed through the metal roof, I could actually see inside the roof metal. I could see the imperfection of the metal—it was like looking and at the same time being inside the metal. After my head rose above the roof, my hands had been on the steering wheel, so they were the next thing I saw—they were OK, but my sleeve was all white, covering my arm. I looked up as I ascended, descending on the rays of the golden sunlight was a man dressed in white with a gold sash down his chest, across and around his waist, with his arms outstretched toward me, coming down to meet me in the air as I rose to meet him.

At that moment, I found myself back in my bed in Blue Springs. I knew something special had just happened to me, but since I didn't understand exactly what it was, I kept the vision to myself and went on about my life, not telling anyone about it until I met my future wife, Kay, years later. She was a Christian and had been born again when she was eight years old. She knew the Bible well, so when she said that only those who had received Christ as their savior and asked forgiveness for their sins would go to heaven, I would argue with her that if anyone was going to heaven, it would be me because I had seen this man dressed in white and had risen to meet him in the air.

She told me that if I didn't know Christ personally, I would bust hell wide open—she didn't pull any punches. (Nice future wife, huh?)

But I am getting ahead of my story. After living in Blue Springs, Missouri, until 1975, I moved to Springfield, Missouri, about 150 miles southeast of Kansas City. My sister, Victoria, and her husband had settled in Springfield to repair mobile homes for insurance companies in the area and had invited me to come and stay with them until I found a job I liked. Since I had never been south of the place of my birth, Sedalia, Missouri, more than thirty miles, it would be an exciting place for me to explore and live.

1 Corinthians 15:51

Now when I speak of Springfield, Missouri, most people do not even know where it's at on the map, but if I mention Branson, Missouri, about thirty miles south of Springfield on Route 65, they or most of my readers would recognize its location. This is important, because after moving to Springfield and making my first trip to Branson, I was reliving my vision of the rapture as I passed through the beautiful hills on Highway 65 on my way to Branson. It was like, at any moment, the clouds could roll back, and I would be changed and rise out of the vehicle. Every time I now make the trip toward Branson, I do so with an expectant heart, ready to hear the trumpets' sound.

Now to fully understand the importance of this vision that God gave to me to share with you, as Paul Harvey, the great radio commentator, used to say, "You haven't heard the rest of the story yet!"

After moving to Springfield in 1975, I was trying to figure out what to do with my life. My sister allowed me to stay with them until I could find something financially rewarding. Sales had always been the vocation that I trained for, for most of my short life before this time. I started real-estate school in 1976 hoping to become a millionaire overnight in land investments even though I didn't have two nickels to rub together at the time.

My brother-in-law had an opportunity to buy ten old used mobile homes in my hometown of Sedalia, Missouri, and asked me to partner up with him. We would bring them back to Springfield, fix them up, and sell them at a profit. My job was to advertise, meet the people, and sell or close the deals, and we would split the profit.

This didn't work out exactly how I expected, but it did get me started in the mobile-home business, where I eventually met my future wife, Kay, in 1977. She was my sister's (Victoria's) beautician, and she had invited her to come home with her to meet her handsome brother—*me*. Ha-ha.

Well, you can guess the rest; we were married on December 3, 1980.

Our son, Justin, was born a year later—December 5, 1981. I also had a stepdaughter, Tonyja, who was twelve at the time of our marriage.

I share this background with you so you'll understand what took place in the near future, in 1983.

For the next two years, from 1981 to 1983, Kay began to go to church steadily every Sunday morning and evening and night. I just could not understand what was so fun or important to attend a religious service that many times, so I started going with her on Sunday morning just to make sure everything was on the up-and-up. We would get to church, and people would hug you and tell you how much they loved you in the Lord and how glad they were to see you. The pastor would stand by the front door and shake your hand and tell you how much he personally appreciated you coming to the service and always invited you back that evening. I always dressed up in one of my fancy suits to let them know I was just as good as they were and that I could say amen and hug them also.

I had always heard that most preachers and churches were just after your money, so be sure to hang on to your wallet, but the strangest thing about this church was most of the people dressed nice, but some wore blue jeans or dress slacks—nice but down-to-earth—and they really seemed sincere when they hugged you and told you they appreciated you being there.

After going to church off and on for about two years, acting like I fit in and was just as good as everyone else, an unexpected event happened to me one night on March 27, 1983.

My wife had made me promise to attend church with her and my son, Justin, and daughter, Tonyja, that Sunday morning on the twenty-seventh.

Since I had been out with my friends Saturday, the night before, I really was in no mood to go to church, but because I had given my word, I forced myself out of bed. I took a shower, dressed, and was ready to go on time. The service was traditional with praise and worship, sharing of God's Word, and a lot of hugging and thanking all for being there, ministering and praying for people at the end of service, and inviting everyone to come back for the evening service.

I had no intention of coming back to the evening service. My head was still hurting from partying the night before. Resting and sleeping were my goals for the next two days and nights.

But as fate (God's intervention) would have it, when we got into our car to leave, one of the visiting college students from Columbia, Missouri, had carried my son, Justin (one year old), out to the car, and as we put him in the backseat to leave, he came around the car to shake my hand and begged me to come back that evening and bring little Justin back so he could see him one more time before he went back to Columbia. My body said no, but my mind was saying yes, and pretty soon, that's what came out of my mouth as I told him we would be back that evening.

Needless to say, I rested most of that Sunday afternoon and felt really good when we went back to attend the Sunday evening service. They had mentioned on Sunday morning that the pastor would not be preaching but they were all going to get together to have a singing celebration to the Lord—everyone was invited to sing and share. So I felt safe to come and relax, be part of the crowd, fit in, and not be noticed. Around 7:00 p.m., they started singing and praising the Lord; everyone was joining in and having a joyful time. This continued for twenty to twenty-five minutes. My wife, Kay, stood on my right side; we were about four rows back from the front in the middle of the congregation. When they begin to sing a worship song called "It's Beginning to Rain," almost everyone had their hands lifted up and their eyes closed as they worshipped the Lord. As I looked around, a strange thing began to happen to me. Tears began to come out of my eyes, and I could not shut them off; I thought if I closed them, maybe it would stop. When I shut my eyes, immediately I was transported in the spirit to a place that looked like a narrow road surrounded by stone walls and buildings. In the middle of this street, there was a man down on one knee with a bark of a tree that was eight to ten inches wide and ten to twelve feet long over his right shoulder. Blood and dirt was running down his face because of the thorns piercing his head. His back was ripped open like you would fillet a fish—the tree bark was crushing down into the cuts—and I was thinking how much pain he must be feeling. When he turned his head toward me, his eyes looked over the tree he was packing directly into mine, and it was like a river of love had hit me. Wave after wave of love began to fill my being. I had never experienced this kind of love before. You can love your father and mother, brothers and sisters, even your wife and children, and still this love would be greater than any other. As I was going through these emotions, the scene in the street changed. It was like when you were a kid and you played with a View-Master—a wheel picture toy wherein every time you clicked it, the picture would change and rotate. The scene changed, and the man kneeling in the street was now lying on his back on these two crossed trees with a man standing over him, nailing his wrist to the cross tree with big spiky-looking nails. Blood was gushing out, and I thought of how much pain he must be going through. I looked from his wrist back to his eyes, and that love once again began to wash over me as it flooded me once again. The scene changed, and I was standing on a hill.

There were two other crosses and men hanging there, but my eyes went to the middle cross. As soldiers dropped the cross in a hole, jarring the man nailed to it, I thought that must really hurt, so I looked up to his eyes once again, and that wave of love washed through my soul. His eyes never left me this time, but it was as if he projected himself off the cross and came down even with me, and both of us went down into the bowels of the earth. We entered the biggest cavern I had ever seen; it looked to be a mile high and spread out for miles. Thousands of people were there. This man that was on the cross was now dressed in all white, standing on a high flat platform (a rock shelf) and speaking to them. I was about ten feet behind him, watching, when he raised his hands high in the air. Everyone in that place began to rise up out of there—myself included!

This next scene was the most beautiful place I had ever seen. We were up on a pure-white rock cliff overlooking a beautiful green valley.

Two gates at least two hundred feet high opened with a wall about two hundred feet high. Running for miles and coming down the valley were thousands of people dancing, holding hands, skipping, playing, and laughing as they entered through these beautiful gates like a bunch of children on their way home after a day of picnicking. It went on for a long time. The man dressed in white on the cliff kept waving them in until, finally, the last *one* went in. I was standing about ten or fifteen feet behind him as the last person went through the gate. The most awful feeling I had ever felt washed over me. It was as if there was darkness, loss, loneliness, separation, and despair in that split second of knowing that I had not entered those gates—"lostness." He turned with his hand pointed at me, and with those same eyes of love, he turned and pointed to the wall. On top of the great wall was a big open book. On the right side, about halfway down, written in bold letters, was my name—Richard Edward Weathers.

I found myself back in that little church standing with tears rolling down my face. The congregation was still singing "It's Beginning to Rain." What seemed to me an hour or so was but a few seconds of time in this world. The Lord had taken me down the road of Via Dolorosa. I watched them crucify him, hang him on a cross, and I became a witness of his death, burial, and resurrection.

What seemed to be a moment of time in this world was, in reality, eternity opening up its arms and inviting me to come in and embrace the love and forgiveness that this person that had died on the cross for me was offering. He took my place, suffered for me, and paid a price with his sinless blood that I could not pay.

Acts 4:12

He gave his all so I could live. I knew then that his name was Jesus, the one and only true God who truly came to this earth to save us from our sins, the son of the living God.

I felt as if a touch of purity had washed over my spirit, cleansing it from all darkness, demons, and unclean spirits, renewing it fresh and clean. My soul (mind) was flooded with the emotion of God's love—a love that goes beyond the world's knowledge of love. It overpowers you with brokenness of self, no longer concerning yourself with the cares of this world but now yielding yourself totally into God's care and hands. It's kind of like jumping off a ten-story building knowing that God truly has you safely in his hands.

John 10:29

And nothing can any longer hurt you, not even death.

Finding myself back in this service with all that I had now experienced, tears running down my face, the pride of who I thought I was in this world was now gone. Standing in its place was now a man who knew that he was a nobody—a sinner that had been lost for eternity—but because of the precious blood of the Lamb, my name had been written in his book, and he loved me so much he had given me an opportunity to accept or reject what he had done for me and the entire world. Standing there broken, I said, "Yes, Lord, save me! A nobody."

While the congregation was still singing, I walked up to the altar, bowed down on my knees, and let his wonderful love wash over me, through me, until it filled every cell in my being—spiritual, mental, and physical. No one led me through a sinner's prayer that night, but they prayed for my family and me.

2 Corinthians 5:17

When I left the altar that night, March 27, 1983, at 7:30 p.m., a new creation in Christ was born of the spirit of God.

After I got home that evening, the first thing I did was remove all booze and every unclean thing that was in my house. God had cleansed my body, his temple, and I (1 Cor. 3:16) cleaned out the one the Holy Spirit would live in.

I was so full of the love of God that every time I went to church, all I could see in my brothers and sisters in the Lord was how beautiful and sinless they were. It was great to be around them and listen to them talk about the things of God. They would all share about the good things that the Lord was doing in their lives. I would ask all kinds of questions concerning different subjects of doctrines, and they would be patient, trying to instruct me with the Word of God. I knew the Lord had called me into the ministry that night he saved me, so Kay and myself began looking for a college to attend and formal training.

But before I go on, let's return for a moment and discuss the vision of the rapture that God had given me ten years before I was saved or born again in that little church at Elwood, Missouri. Living in that house in Blue Springs, I had no formal church upbringing or study of God's Word other than the few times growing up as a boy around nine or ten years of age that our mother made us attend a little church called Olive Branch Baptist Church at Beaman, Missouri, just outside of Sedalia.

Somewhere during this time, God seeded his Word in me even though I couldn't quote a scripture, not even John 3:16.

Romans 5:9
1 Thessalonians 5:9
Revelation 3:10

God gave me this vision so you would know that he truly is coming in my generation to take all his children out of this world back to heaven before his wrath is let loose on this earth. You will not be here during the tribulation period of seven years that will be poured out on the earth. There are people teaching of a mid—or posttribulation rapture, and even though I love them in the Lord, they are wrong in their interpretations of God's Word.

1 Thessalonians 5:11

God instructed us to comfort each other and edify one another with the word of his coming back for us.

Revelation 6:1
Revelation 6:8

There's not much comfort when we teach that we all will face the twenty-one judgments of God in the book of Revelation. Most of us will be beheaded for the gospel's sake. One-fourth of mankind will be killed under the Seal Judgments alone.

No! My friends, God will not pour his wrath out on his body, his beloved bride, but will deliver us to heaven before even the Antichrist can be revealed.

2 Thessalonians 2:3
2 Timothy 1:7

God did not give us a spirit of fear so that we would cower down at the thought of God beating us up or putting sickness or disease on us for not living up, somehow, to his expectations. In James 1:23 it says, "Let no one say (this includes some so-called preachers) when he is tested or tempted." I am tested by God. God cannot be tempted or tested by evil, nor does he himself tempt anyone.

You have nothing to prove to God by going through the tribulation period, trying to show how strong you are, how you can endure pain and suffering for Jesus. God does not have to test you for you to be more godly or faithful.

John 5:24
Ephesians 4:24
Colossians 2:8
1 Corinthians 11:16

The moment you put your faith in Jesus and his Word on the cross, you pass from death in this world to life with him in his kingdom. It's not through our religious works that anyone will get to heaven but only through our faith in his completed work on the cross. There are those who believe that only a few holier-than-thou Christians (usually like them) will make the first rapture, and the rest of us will be left to continue our struggle to perfect holiness according, of course, to their definition of true holiness—not God's, but through their religious works of how good you are—being at church on time, never missing a Sunday service, giving your tithe without fail, obeying their every command (because it comes straight from God, and only they really hear from God, so they know best), not eating certain foods or wearing certain clothes, not wearing makeup and being sure the women never cut their hair.

It all sounds like God, but the truth is the Lord came to set us free of all these bondages (Rom. 8:1). There is no condemnation to those that are in Christ Jesus—whom the Son sets free is free indeed (John 8:36).

So who will go to heaven when the trumpets sound? All that are in Christ Jesus (1 Cor. 15:51)—that means every one of us that knows Jesus Christ as our personal savior, everyone who has asked Jesus to forgive them of their sins shall be saved. We will go on the first load to be with the king forever.

God gave me the vision of the catching-away of his church in 1973, ten years before I would be born again in 1983, to be able to understand his Word through the Holy Spirit that was now in me, teaching and showing me revelation. At the time God gave me this vision, I did not understand it, but I knew something supernatural had happened to me because I was part of it and felt and experienced the emotions of being there in person. John 14:26

1 Corinthians 15:51-52

The Lord knew that I was not in bondage to man's doctrines or religious in my thinking, but my mind (soul) would be a clean slate for him and the Holy Spirit to take me into the future and allow me to see and experience my own rapture as he personally came back for his bride, his body, his church. Every person in Christ will personally be received by Christ himself; they will all feel his love as he comes back for all of us when the trumpet sounds. Now let's examine a little closer the vision and what was happening at the time it took place.

The first thing you should know was that, number 1, it was a beautiful day—no bombs were falling on the USA, no fear of plagues including Covid totally wiping us out, no war inside the United States that would have disrupted commerce. It was a day like any other day you experience. People were driving their cars in an orderly manner on the highways, it was calm and relaxing, there was a beautiful, clear blue sky—a wonderful day of peace.

Revelation 6:8
Revelation 8:7
Revelation 9:15

The reason the Lord impressed the quietness of the day upon me was so I would realize when the word was revealed about when the rapture would take place. I would know that it would be before the seven-year tribulation period was poured out upon the earth, before the Seal Judgments could be loosed that destroy mankind, before the Trumpet Judgments that destroy one-third of the earth and water, before the Vial Judgment that would be poured out on the seat of Satan (Rev. 16:2).

1 Thessalonians 5:9
Hebrews 9:22

God wanted to assure me that he would come for us before that great and terrible time of his wrath, which will be loosed upon the earth because of sinful man's rebellion against him. They rejected his plan of salvation (2 Thess. 2:11), so they will have to pay the price and feel his wrath. A strong delusion to believe a lie has already started to blind the minds of men to receive any religion as truth but reject the Son of God that was sent to die for them and anything that has to do with Christianity. There are those today that believe they are Christians but that it's OK to abort babies and promote homosexuality, that basically all religions and beliefs are OK because all religions will one day all lead to God, that there are many different ways to be saved (John 14:6) and we all just go up the mountain through different paths (Acts 4:12). How sad for these folks, who are good people, believing that because God is love, there is no hell or final judgment for anyone as long as you do good and love everybody, that all will be well with your soul, and God will allow you to come into his heaven because he is fair. The problem with this thinking is God is also a god of judgment. Everyone, someday, will have to stand before God and give an account of his life, either good or bad (2 Cor. 5:10), but we cannot enter heaven because of good works (Eph. 2:8, Gal. 2:16). It will only be by the grace of God through faith in Jesus Christ and his works of righteousness on the cross that we can be saved (Rom. 10:9-10). We cannot enter heaven any other way; there is no other salvation or name on earth or in heaven given to us to be saved (Acts 4:12). The lie from Satan that because you belong to the chosen church or because you act holy or because you're baptized by a certain man of God or because someone sealed you with the Holy Spirit for salvation or because they wrote your name in what they call their book of life of the saved—you are not! It was the blood of Jesus only that was shed for the remission of your sins, and only the blood of Jesus can wash them away. You must be born again (John 3:5) of water (Eph. 5:26), the Word, and the Spirit (Holy Spirit) of God. This is an individual or personal commitment each one of us must make to God.

Romans 10:9-10

We must personally confess with our mouths and believe in our hearts that God sent his only begotten son (Jesus) to die for us, and through his death, burial, and resurrection, we can have eternal life in him.

Titus 2:13

The second thing God impressed upon me when he gave me the vision was the peace I felt as the clouds rolled back and the angels appeared to sound the trumpets. As it all unfolded before my eyes, a calmness took over my mind, and it was as if this was the most natural thing in the world to be happening. Yet there was an exciting expectancy of this event.

When Jesus appeared all dressed in white with the gold sash coming down his chest and round his waist, his arms outstretched to receive me in his arms, I now realize that Jesus was coming, like he promised, to take his bride, his body, home with him (John 14:2) to his father's house, where we will all be with him for eternity. This is not an event where we need to hide out in caves, starving for lack of food and water, waiting for the terrible wrath of God to be finished and finally do its destructive work on earth, living with a spirit of fear that we will be beheaded at any moment because we had refused to take the mark of the Beast (Rev 13:16-17). No! God has promised us that he would not give us a spirit of fear but of power, love, and sound mind (2 Tim. 1:7).

Take my word for it (as a Christian psychologist)—your mind or body would not be very sound if you had to live through the tribulation period. God did not appoint us to his wrath (1 Thess. 5:9) but to obtain salvation through our Lord, Jesus Christ.

Let this be the day you truly trust Jesus for deliverance—of your spirit, soul, and body—and know that he not only forgave you of your sins, but one day he will also bring deliverance to your body, and it will be changed in a fraction of a second (1 Cor. 15:51), and you will experience the power of the peace he has for you (John 16:33). I John 3:2

1 Corinthians 15:52

The third thing you need to be aware of is that when the Lord comes back for his church, no one will see him unless he belongs to him. On the day the trumpets sound, only the redeemed shall see and hear him. To the world of unbelievers, you will just disappear right in front of them—so fast in a twinkling of an eye, you will vanish before them. Your jewelry and clothes will be left behind on the ground, but you and your bones will be gone.

1 Thessalonians 5:2

Like a thief in the night, he will come for us. The world will not know what has happened to their loved ones. They'll look everywhere trying to find them but to no avail. Voices will rise up proclaiming they know what has happened—aliens from outer space have taken them or God has gotten rid of the troublemakers that have held the world back from advancing its goals of brotherhood where everyone can get along. Now a new-world order of love and order can take place, where everyone shall have peace and safety and prosperity. The new messiah shall step forward with all the right answers for the world's problems. The world shall now open its borders to all nations and become one with the people. There shall be no more walls to hold each other out, but a world leader that has broken down the barriers that have kept different nationalities out will form a one-world government made up of ten different continents ruled by governors or kings. Under the command of this elected world leader, a world passport—one card—will be issued to all citizens so they can travel anywhere anytime. This card will allow them to operate for the first three and a half years in the new economic system that will be developed. It will be accepted by all nations and authorities. A new currency will be developed, but it will not be a cash currency—it will be a credit/debit system. All dollar credits will be electronically put in your account, which banks will begin to provide to all people and nations, free of charge, to be issued using the same number that will be on your world passport card. This number will be assigned as a life number that only you (while you are alive) will use. This will look good for the first three and a half years into the rule of the Antichrist. By then, the whole world of people will be on electronic records in computers, and all their information will be tracked and recorded. But what about the last three and a half years of this evil man's rule?

Let's go back for just a moment to where this rapture takes place so that we can explain why these things will unfold after Jesus comes back for his bride.

1 Thessalonians 4:13
Revelation 19:11
Isaiah 28:11

After being born again in 1983, the Lord put in my heart to study his Word, especially prophecy and the book of Revelation, so when this day would come, we could put down in writing the vision of his coming for his people in two phases of the second coming—first in the air to take out all Christians before the seven years of tribulation, and the second, coming back to earth with his saints to take control of the earth (his kingdom). I have spent thousands of hours in God's Word of prophecy and in prayer to understand the mind and will of God in these last days. Twenty-seven books of the Old Testament and seventeen books of the New Testament tie directly into the book of Revelation written by John the Apostle around AD 96. If the Word of God is taken literally and studied with common sense, and we can believe God to say what he means and believe he can keep his promise and does not lie (Rom. 3:4), then the Word of God can make clear sense—line upon line, precept upon precept. The scriptures cannot be broken (John 10:35) but will deliver exactly what God has spoken about the past, present, and future. There were over three hundred prophecies in the Old Testament predicting the coming of Jesus. They were all fulfilled at the perfect timing of God Almighty. Most of God's saints know of these scriptures beginning in Genesis 3:15—putting enmity between Satan and the seed of woman where Jesus would eventually come, finally bruising Satan's head, taking back the authority over the earth he stole (he would bruise his head or put him on the cross to be crucified) or the scripture in Isaiah 53:4-6 where it described his crucifixion or Psalms 22:1 when he cried out from the cross, "My God, my God, why have you forsaken me?" These scriptures were fulfilled completely at the right time and place.

The future prophecies of God's words will also be fulfilled. Daniel 9:26-27 says there will be a coming Roman prince (Antichrist) that will sign a seven-year peace treaty with the nation of Israel six hundred years before Israel was scattered by the Romans in power in AD 70 and two thousand years later, when God brought them back in their land on May 14, 1948.

Matthew 24:34

There has never been a seven-year peace treaty with the nation of Israel in over 2,550 years. But in our generation, the world will become part of seeing one take place as the Antichrist rises out of the old Roman Empire (the European common-market countries) and signs this treaty with Israel. It will be the beginning of the last seven years of man's rule on earth. It will begin the worst time man has ever experienced on earth—wars, famines, earthquakes, floods, hail, fire and brimstone, death and disease all around them, the wrath of God poured out on all those who have rejected his son, Jesus, and his way of salvation (John 14:6). Within a seven-year period, over one-half of the world's population will die. According to Revelation 6:8, one-fourth of all the population will suffer) and Rev 9:15.

There are now around seven billion people on earth (as of this writing). Let's assume one billion are raptured at the coming of Jesus in the air; this will still be six billion people on earth at the beginning of the tribulation period. According to the Bible, three billion will die before Jesus comes back with his saints (Rev. 19:11, Jude 1:14) to take control of the earth before mankind wipes itself out (Matt. 24:22)—that's about ten times the population of the USA now at three hundred fifty million.

CHAPTER 2

GOD'S TIME LINE FOR THE RAPTURE

There is always order in how God has created the earth and all that dwell in it. The sun is not too close to burn us up or too far away to freeze us to death. He even hung out the moon at the right distance to centralize our oceans and seas by magnetic force so, like a bowl of water, it keeps the oceans' waters from spilling out and overflowing onto the shores. You and I can't even walk across a room with a cup full of water without spilling some with the earth rotating around on its axis every twenty-four hours, but the oceans' waters do not move out of their boundaries.

To the last inch—from the trees and animals to the air we breathe, God has provided for every need in our life here to survive. Every element, from water, heat, shelter, food, and the clothes we wear, he has given it to us. The birds and all animals have homes and food; this is not by accident but the way God has set up the order of the universe.

Have you ever thought of what would have happened after Adam and Eve sinned in the garden if God had just said, "Let's wipe out this mistake and start all over with a new species other than mankind we created in our own image"?

But God didn't do that because the truth is, God doesn't make mistakes.

He already knew man would fail the test in the garden and that his son, the Lord Jesus, would have to die for the sins of mankind (Eph. 1:4, 2 Tim. 1:9), and *before time began* and his creation of the earth, God already put in order all that would be needed to fulfill his will on earth as it is in heaven (Matt. 6:10).

To understand the full scope of man's salvation and deliverance and the situation we find ourselves in today, we have to go back before time began and look into heaven as a rebellion was taking place against God.

Ezekiel 28:12

One of God's chief archangels, Lucifer, was plotting an overthrow of heaven (Isa. 14:12-14). He wanted to ascend above God, sit in rule over God's creations. He was the Son of the Morning and already had the highest position in heaven to bring praise and worship to God. He walked in the midst of fiery stones before God. He was the seal of perfections, full of wisdom and perfect in beauty; every precious stone was his covering. But what changed a perfect angel into a rebellious devil?

Lucifer was the fourth most powerful authority in the kingdom, just under God the Father, Son, and the Holy Spirit of God. He enjoyed this position of "praise leader," but something happened that changed him. God said he was perfect up until iniquity (pride) was found in him. I believe God's Word gives us a clue to what happened. All was well in heaven until God made the declaration that he was going to make man in his image (Gen. 1:26) and he would give man authority or dominion over all the birds and animals and the earth itself.

Lucifer realized that God was creating sons and daughters to rule the earth and, eventually, all of God's kingdom, and he would also have to bow down and be under the authority of the sons of the kingdom.

Now this is right out of the "book of Rick." You will have to pray and let the Holy Spirit show you this truth of this revelation or let it roll off you and love me anyway.

Lucifer knew that instead of being the fourth most powerful being in God's kingdom, he would now just be an angel that would be under the command of God's children. He was perfect up until this announcement, and that's when, I believe, pride came into his heart. Anger began to consume him, and he took one-third of the angels in heaven under his command and tried to rebel against God.

There was war in the heaven before time *on earth* began. Lucifer and his angels were cast out of the physical heaven into the void or space.

God went ahead and created the earth and all within, separated the heavens and air in the atmosphere around the earth, divided the oceans and the seas, made mankind (set up the Garden of Eden), and made ready the test of mankind that would also eventually judge Lucifer, now called Satan, after being cast out of the first heaven to the second heaven where the stars and planets are. We must understand that in God's kingdom, there was no sin, no reason for a judgment wherein someone could be cast out of the kingdom from the presence of God forever.

After, God gave man dominion over the entire earth and all within.

Matthew 25:41

Satan waited for his opportunity to deceive Eve because she heard God give the command to Adam to eat of every tree but not the Tree of Good and Evil (Gen. 2:17) because the day they ate of it, they would surely die. This was the first mention in God's Word that death could occur. Before this, death and judgment had no real meaning to angels in heaven. It was hard for them to understand why God had to kick out Satan and one-third of the angels, now demons (1 Pet. 1:11-12). Now the angels looked into the plan of salvation, and they now began to understand why God had to judge Satan and all the fallen angels and why man himself would also suffer the judgment that God had set up for just Satan and his demons (Isa. 14:9, Ps. 9:17).

God allowed man to make his own choice to either obey or disobey in the garden. He told him the day he ate would also be the day he died. His spiritual connection with a pure, sinless God was severed the moment he disobeyed God and ate of the Tree of Good and Evil. He didn't die physically—his mind or soul didn't stop working—it was his spirit-to-spirit relationship to God that died. God no longer could speak with Adam from the inside out. Communications now would be from the outside in—the five physical senses of man (hearing, seeing, smelling, tasting, touching). God now would begin talking and helping man from the outside of his kingdom. Satan, that day, stole the right from Adam to become the prince of this world (2 Cor. 4) to try to keep it in darkness and control man through his evil spirits.

But God already knew the plan of Satan, and he has used every move to bring a full judgment to him and his demons.

We see how God began his plan in Genesis 3:15 to bring forth his seed, and he will take back what Satan had stole that day.

God saw how Satan polluted the earth and man's minds with wickedness, so God destroyed the earth with a flood but chose Noah and his sons and wives to walk up right before him in a new beginning. Gen 6:8-9

Later, after more people were born on the earth, God called out Abraham and cut a covenant with him. (A covenant is simply a binding agreement between two partners.) Since God was one of the partners, it would be an unbreakable contract. God told Abraham that through his seed, all nations would be blessed, and anyone who blessed him would be blessed (Gen. 12:2). Today we know that seed was Jesus, who would die and save us from our sins, and we would be born again into the household of God (Gal. 3:29). Through Abraham, Isaac and Jacob would have twelve sons, and each one would become a tribe, and all of these would become the nation of Israel that God would call *his people*, the Jews, to love and protect until they disobeyed him. He set up his laws for them to live by and also to teach them that no person was perfect or righteous but that all have sinned and fallen short of God's glory and righteousness (Rom. 3:23).

This brings us back to why God has provided a time line to the Rapture of the Church.

Daniel 9:2
Jeremiah 25:12-14

In the Old Testament, God brought judgment to the nation of Israel for their disobedience of his Holy Sabbath (Lev. 25:1-4). They planted crops in the seventh year when they were supposed to let it rest. God pronounced seven times' return on the seventy years they were in disobedience—that would be 70 × 7 = 490 years they would have to pay God back in tribulation. Daniel speaks of the seventy years that Daniel knew was just about up from the time of captivity by Nebuchadnezzar in 606 BC. He figured out that this was almost over in his time of capture and would be up in 536 BC. Daniel repented for the nation (Dan. 9:15-16) to turn back God's anger from Israel. God gave Daniel a vision and sent Gabriel to give him the ability to understand the vision even though seventy years of original judgment were up.

God had pronounced a seventy-by-seven-year judgment, and God wanted Daniel to understand it wasn't over yet but still to be fulfilled in the future when it would begin the going forth of the command to rebuild the temple in Jerusalem (Dan. 9:28) and the time that the Messiah would be cut off or crucified in AD 32. It would be seven weeks plus sixty-two weeks for a total of sixty-nine weeks or 483 years because of the Jews' rejection of their messiah (Jesus). God stopped the ticking of the judgment-time clock on them and began a new dispensation called the Age of Grace (Eph. 3:2). It would be a time that whosoever would believe in Christ as their personal savior (John 3:16) would be saved. The new covenant of grace would not be who had the most money or who worked harder in the kingdom of God, but it would be by faith alone (Eph. 2:8) in Christ Jesus and the works he had done on the cross of Calvary by himself. There would be no salvation in any other religious work or way, only through the name and blood of Jesus (Acts 4:12). John 6:28

Matthew 28:18

For two thousand years, the body or bride of Christ has been born or birthed into the kingdom of God. We alone have been given the great commission of preaching God's Word throughout the world. The Holy Spirit that has made us new creations in Christ Jesus has also taught us God's Word, trained us how to use the Word in the kingdom, and has led and guided us on our mission to win souls while we are on this earth. II Cor 5:21

But soon our ministries on earth will be finished, and the Lord will begin a new work (Rom. 11:1), once again dealing with the nation of Israel (Abraham's physical seed) to bring them back into the fold to accept Jesus as the real Messiah and begin preaching that the kingdom is coming. Up to now it makes no difference whether you were a Jew or Gentile, man or woman, slave or free person (Gal. 3:28). God saves all of us through the shed blood of his son, Jesus.

Before Jesus died for the whole world to be saved, only the Jews that were in covenant with God could be saved. They would sacrifice a calf or goat once a year in their temple in the holy of holies. The priest would take the innocent blood of the animal, sprinkle it on the altar of the holy ark, and their sins would be passed over or forgiven for one more year. This went on until Jesus came and was crucified on the cross; God has offered forgiveness to the world if they would but believe in Christ and call out for salvation (Rom. 10:9-10).

The truth is, more people are going into *hell* than heaven. The pride in man has kept him from bowing his knee to God's only way of salvation through his son. They want to come up with their own way of coming to God. Some think hard work is the answer. Others embrace cults and religious works or baptism and their ways of holiness. Still others follow men that claim to be Christ or God—false prophets, the Bible says, are twice dead (Jude 1:12), the blind leading the blind. As the coming of Christ back to earth draws nearer, more and more cults and deceivers will come forth proclaiming to be Christ and that *only they* have the way back to God—that only by following them or becoming part of their group will you be able to ever see God. More later on this.

The Jews that were in covenant with God refused to accept Jesus as their messiah two thousand years ago when he came and presented himself to them. The Pharisees rejected Jesus because to accept meant confessing that Jesus truly was the Son of God (Isa. 7:14), the promised son that would be born, and his name would be Immanuel or "God with us." Even after Jesus raised Lazarus from the dead after four days in the grave—a notable miracle—they sought to kill not only Jesus but also Lazarus (John 12:10).

They loved their position and the praises of men (John 12:43) more than the praise of God. So all the Jewish people paid the price in AD 70. Titus of the Roman Empire came into Jerusalem and destroyed the city and tore down the temple of Solomon and scattered the Jews around the world. The Jewish people had not been back in their homeland as a nation in over 2,500 years, but in our generation, on May 14, 1948, God brought forth the Jewish nation of Israel once again and put his people, the physical seed of Abraham, back into their promised homeland (Isa 66:8). He also said in his Word that the generation that saw these things happening would not pass away before he came back to the earth (Matt. 24:34). Everyone born in 1948 still living on earth will witness his coming. The closing out of this age of grace is already upon us, and the ushering in of the age of peace and the Messiah's rule, a one-thousand-year reign, will take place shortly.

There is an order of events that will unfold according to God's plan of redemption for mankind.

Daniel 9:24

I said earlier that God had pronounced judgment on the nation of Israel for 490 years with 483 of those years fulfilled upon the crucifixion of Jesus. About two thousand years have passed since his resurrection and ascension to heaven (Acts 1:9). They saw him taken up, and a cloud received him out of their sight. In verse 11, two angels told them that in like manner, this same Jesus would return as you saw him go into heaven.

This is important because when Christ returns to earth, there will be two returns—one for his church or body still on this earth to meet them in the air where all born-again believers in Christ in heaven and here will be united as one with Christ (Eph. 1:10, 1 Cor. 15:51-52), where we will be taken into heaven for seven years to have our seven-year wedding feast to be married officially to the Lamb of God (Rev. 3:10). Matt 22:1-13

God has given his church a promise to keep them from (*ek*, "out of " in Greek) the hour of trial that will come upon the earth to try the whole world. God has not appointed his bride to the wrath of God (Rom. 5:9). There are those in the body who try to teach that there is no such doctrine as a rapture in the Bible, and still others teach that there will be a catching-away, but it will not take place until the end of the tribulation period when Jesus comes back on the last day—then we will be changed, rise to meet him in the air, turn right around, and immediately come back to earth. It all sounds good until you actually study God's Word and find to believe these teachings, you would have to deny too many other scriptures to make them work without breaking his word. Jesus said in John 10:35 that his scriptures could not be broken. What he was saying is that his Word, the entire book of the Bible, must flow in conjunction with all other scriptures (2 Pet. 1:19-21). There is no private interpretation, and if a doctrine does not fit, we need to keep studying until it does.

For example, there are those that teach that God no longer heals people and there aren't any miracles being performed today for people that need them; they have all passed away with the original apostles. If that was the case, the greatest miracle of all—called the new birth (to be born again in Christ)—could not take place in our hearts. All sins to be forgiven and a new creation in Christ (2 Cor. 5:17) could not happen, but praise God, he still saves and he still heals. Just because some well-meaning soul teaches error and says this is the way, it is does not make it so. All of God's Word must fit into the whole picture of God's plan and word of truth.

At the time of Jesus's death two thousand years ago, the plan for Israel was put on hold, and the grace of God was poured out upon the world so millions could come to Christ through the cross. But the time of grace that has formed the body of Christ is almost over, and God will go back to dealing with Israel to bring them to their messiah (Jesus), whom they rejected as savior two thousand years ago.

How will God accomplish this? Since only the church has been given the commission of preaching the gospel to the world (Matt. 28:18).

God has set up an *exit plan* for the church before he begins dealing with Israel to bring them back to him through Christ (Rom. 11:1-2). That plan is called the Rapture of the Church (1 Thess. 4:17) or the catching-away of his bride. There are several reasons why this must happen before God deals with the Jewish people. The body of Christ must be gone from the earth so God can finish his judgment on Israel

(Dan. 9:27) to complete the 490 years pronounced in Daniel's time. One more week or seven years are left to be fulfilled. According to Daniel 9:27, this week will begin with the signing of a seven-year peace treaty with the man called the Antichrist, a person that will be raised up out of the old Roman Empire and be in power over the European common-market countries already formed today.

God will go back to a 360-day year. So from the beginning to the end of what is called the tribulation period, there will be 2,520 days before Christ returns to earth to take control of his earth and kingdom. The first three and a half years of the tribulation period will be a lesser tribulation where Israel goes back to a time of peace and rebuilds their holy temple to restart physical animal sacrifices as they did in the old days before the temple was destroyed in AD 70. Jesus taught that after three and a half years, the Antichrist (Matt. 24:15) will break the peace agreement and set himself up as God in their holy place in the temple and become the "abomination of desolation." He warned his people (the Jews) to flee when they see this happen. According to Zechariah 13:8-9, two-thirds of the people in Jerusalem will die, but God will bring one-third through the fire of tribulation, and they will survive (Dan. 11:41).

Many will flee to Edom, Moab, and Ammon in the country of Jordan out of the hand of the Antichrist. When this happens, the great tribulation, or last three and a half years will begin, a time that Jesus (Matt. 24: 21) said would be so terrible that if he had not shortened the time, all mankind would destroy itself (Matt. 24:22). No flesh would be saved—the tribulation period is not for the church or Christ's body. The wrath of God is not poured out upon his body to teach them something or because he is angry with them; his "wrath" is his anger against all unrighteous people who do not believe the truth of God's son (Eph 2:3).

For two thousand years, we have lifted up the cross and the Son of God as the way of truth and salvation (John 14:6). There is no other way to the Father except by Jesus and his blood. God will remove his bride from this earth before his wrath is poured out on the world; we have not been appointed to this part of God's plan (1 Thess. 5:9). The Lord said through the apostle Paul to comfort each other with this news (1 Thess. 5:11). No one in the body of Christ is trying to escape any tribulation—it's God who is saying he will keep us from this hour of trial (Rev. 3:10), the same great God who saved us from our sins, saves to the uttermost (Heb. 7:25), will also come back in the air (1 Thess. 4:18), and change our corruptible bodies, and we will all rise to meet him in the air. He will bring back all the saints who are in heaven that have gone home before us. They will enter the graves, be changed, and we who are alive shall receive our incorruptible bodies together and go back with Jesus to the Father's house (John 14:2) before the seven years of tribulation begin and before the Antichrist can be revealed (2 Thess. 2:3).

The "falling away" talked about in verse 3 is the word (in Greek) *apostasy*. It also means "departure." When Christ comes back for his church, there will be a disappearance of all saints faster than you can blink your eye (1 Cor. 15:51-52), a departure of millions of born-again believers in Christ will be gone from the world. They will not know what happened to us. They will look all over for us, but we will not be found on earth. We will go to heaven to attend our wedding.

In the Old Testament, a Jewish marriage started with the father of the groom arranging the marriage. He selected a bride who was suitable for his son. Then the son or groom made a proposal to the woman by giving her father and her a marital contract. If accepted, the groom would pour a glass of wine and give it to the woman. If she agreed, she would drink; if not, she would slide it away to wait for someone else.

Christ did the same thing for us in Matthew 26:27-28. He took the cup of wine, gave thanks to God the Father for it, gave it to the disciples, and said, "Each of you drink from it for this is my blood," which confirms the covenant between God and his people.

If the woman accepts the proposal, the groom pays a price for her or a dowry. He gives it to her father. We too were bought at a price with the precious blood of Christ (1 Pet. 1:18-19).

Next, the bridegroom gives gifts to the bride; it shows his appreciation for his bride. They will also help her remember him during the long betrothal period. Christ also has given his bride gifts—the Holy Spirit (John 14:26) to be our guide and teacher (Eph. 4:8).

The couple is now officially betrothed. They separately take a ritual bath as a symbol of spiritual cleansing; she is called his bride, and he is called her bridegroom. They are legally bound together, but it will take another year or two before the marriage can be consummated. The bridegroom and the bride will not see each other during this time. She will wear a veil in public to show the world that she has been taken and she is set apart or sanctified for her future husband. The bride will use this time to make herself ready for the marriage. Just like the church today makes herself ready with the washing of the word (Eph. 5:25) so she also can be presented as his bride.

In a Jewish marriage, the bridegroom begins to prepare a bridal chamber for his new bride in his father's house. This chamber will be the place the bride and bridegroom consummate their marriage and have their honeymoon (John 14:2-3). The Lord said, "In my father's house are many mansions," and he would go and prepare a place for us. Then he said, "Where I am, I will come back and take you to be with me."

After the bridegroom prepares and finishes the bridal chamber, he returns for his bride. She will know of the *general time* of his coming but will not know the *hour* or the *day* he will come. The bridegroom will arrive *in the night* in his best clothes with a crown on his head to take his bride away. The bride will wait every night with her bridesmaids with oil in their lamps for the bridegroom to come (Matt. 24:36). The church does not know the day or the hour when Jesus will come, but one day shortly, in the near future, Jesus will come, and the trumpets will sound (1 Thess. 4:16), and we who are alive shall be changed in a blink of an eye along with the saints he brings back that have already gone home before us. All shall be changed and rise to meet him in the air (raptured).

When the bridegroom and his party are close to the home of the bride, he will utter a shout and blow the trumpet.

The bridegroom will take his bride to the bridal chambers or back to his father's house. The best man will be waiting outside the chambers for the bridegroom to announce the consummation of the marriage, and then the wedding guests will celebrate as they wait inside the house for the bride and bridegroom to leave the chamber (John 3:29).

The bride and bridegroom will stay in the chamber for seven days. After this time, they will come out of the chamber, then the marriage supper will begin with all the wedding guests. The bride is no longer a bride but is now the wife of the bridegroom (Rev. 19:7-9), so it shall be also when, after seven years in heaven with Jesus, we come back at the end of the seven years of tribulation on earth to rule and reign with the Lord for one thousand years, which will be the marriage supper of the Lord and his bride.

What we see in the Jewish marriage is God's plan of marriage for his son, Jesus.

The sovereign father (God) chooses a bride for his son (Jesus). The son leaves the realm unseen and humbles himself to the level of humanity. He pays the dowry price for his bride (his blood and life) so he might raise her up to heavenly realms from which he came. The Holy Spirit (HS) lures, enchants, and captivates the bride by the irresistible beauty of the son.

This is the heart and soul of the sacred romance. All universal history is joyfully awaiting the union of the heavenly bridegroom and his earthly bride. Even Earth groans within itself waiting for the revealing of the sons of God (Rom. 8:19). We are but one shout away from leaving this earth to be with our bridegroom, Jesus.

As I wrote before, the seven days we spend in the bridal chamber represent the seven years we go to be with Jesus in heaven where we will enjoy time with him and all our loved ones that have gone before us. We will experience being in the Father's house (heaven) and meet the Old Testament saints that are there enjoying the fullness of love and peace and a unity of God's spirit that, right now, we only have a little taste of (Eph. 1:13).

In our glorified bodies, bodies like Christ (1 John 3:2), we will be able to move at the speed of thought. Our minds will be opened to receive 100 percent of knowledge and wonderment of God's kingdom. Now most psychologists say studies into our minds show less than 10 percent of our mind power or brain is being used. Our senses of smell, touch, vision, hearing, and even tasting or eating will be enhanced for our enjoyment. Jesus, when he appeared to his disciples in Luke 24:41-43, asked for food. He ate fish and honey to show them he was more than a spirit but flesh and bone. I believe he also enjoyed eating, and he knew we would also in these new bodies.

When we finally get to heaven, God knows it will take billions and billions of years for us to explore, enjoy, and experience all that he has created for us (1 Cor. 2:9).

We get a foretaste of heaven before we come back with Christ to take over the kingdom of the earth. While we will have been having a great time in heaven for seven years, down on Earth there will have been seven years of hell going on called the tribulation period. The tribulation starts with the signing of a peace treaty with Israel for seven years and ends with the coming back of Christ with his saints (us) (Jude 1:14) at the end of the seven years, or 2,520 days from start to finish. He will arrive on the Mount of Olives where his feet will touch, and the mountain will split east and west. The mountain shall move north and south, a great earthquake shall take place, and water shall run out of Jerusalem to the Dead Sea and the Mediterranean, making the Dead Sea and the fish live again (Zech. 14:4-9).

This also causes water to run into the valley of Jezereel, where the armies of the earth are gathered to do war against Christ and the saints. This valley is 14 miles wide and 180 miles long. The Bible tells us in Revelation 14:20 that the blood will rise up to the horses' bridles about five and a half feet tall. A two-hundred-million-man army from the east will be those with the Antichrist's armies, and they will be destroyed by hailstones weighing 100 to 120 pounds, crashing into their armies and smashing them into pulp while water rushing down the valley, mixing with their blood, runs toward the Dead Sea and the Mediterranean, making this valley a river of blood or the winepress of the Lord (Rev. 14:18-19), also called the supper of the Lord where all those that come against him shall be fed to the birds (Rev. 19:17-19). Here in the valley of Megiddo the final battle of the Antichrist shall take place. This will be his last day on top of earth before he and the false prophet are cast into the lake of fire (Rev. 19:20). For all of you that don't believe in a literal hell, you ought to study this scripture and the one in Revelation 20:10 that says after one thousand years, Satan will be released from his holding place or prison to deceive the nation again and gather them from the four corners of the earth to do battle with the saints. They will be destroyed immediately, and Satan will be cast into the lake of fire where the Antichrist and false prophet will have been for one thousand years in torment. This is the only other choice for those who reject Jesus, the only way of salvation.

Romans 11:1

God is a god of order, and everything that will take place from now and into the future has been revealed to his saints. If those that study and show themselves (2 Tim. 2:15) approve, rightly dividing the word (2 Tim. 2:15) of truth (2 Tim. 3:14-16), they will be able to see, through the Holy Spirit, the things that are in their future (John 16:13). The book of Revelation was given to John the revelator to show his servants things that were about to come upon the earth so we could have peace and comfort about our future (1 Thess. 5:11) and be able to comfort others about the coming of the Lord and where this age (age of the church) would fit in his plan as it would come to an end and about a plan to bring the Jewish people back to their Messiah, fulfilling the last seven years of judgment foretold in Daniel 9:26-27, in which God's wrath will be poured out not only on the Jews but also upon the rest of humanity that had rejected his son. There is a dispensational time line that runs throughout the Old and New Testament that shows God using "a day equals a thousand years" (2 Pet. 3:8).

The first dispensation begins in the Garden of Eden as a time of *innocence*, a time where there was no death or sin. God was in constant communication and fellowship by his spirit with Adam and Eve. They were given great power over all the animals and every living creature, dominion to rule the earth as God the Father spoke the world into existence, so Adam and Eve would only have to speak a word, and things would change at their direction. There was peace and wonderment in the Garden of Eden, a contentment of safety that mankind has never yet known. The "spirit world" of God's entire kingdom (heaven)—angels and all spiritual creations of God—was opened to Adam. He could see into this world as clearly as Elisha prayed so his servant could see the armies of heaven that were surrounding the Syrian army (2 Kings 6:16-17).

But Adam was given a command by God not to eat of the fruit of the Tree of Good and Evil. In Genesis 2:17, the day he would eat would also be the day he would die.

After the fall of Adam, man became aware of good and evil. This began the second *dispensation of conscience*, a time when mankind did whatever they felt was right in their own eyes (Gen. 6:5). Their thoughts and the intents of their hearts were evil continually, so God decided to destroy mankind because of their evil cause on earth. But one man found grace and favor with God. Noah and his family—three sons and their wives—would be saved from the destruction or flood that would come upon the earth. He commissioned Noah to build a great ship to house his family and all the animals that would be spared. After the flood, the ark rested on the mountaintops in the country we now know as Turkey. Noah and his sons' families began to multiply in this new world.

And this began the third dispensation of *human government*, a time in which Noah ruled with his family—his sons Shem, Japheth, and Ham—because Ham dishonored his father and saw his nakedness and told his brother outside. They covered him with a garment by walking backward into the tent so they did not see him. Ham received a curse from his father. He would be the father of the Canaanites and be a servant to his brothers. Human government worked all right until Nimrod was born and decided he would build a tower into heaven. The people all had one language at the time and spoke the same speech.

Nimrod convinced them to build a city and a tower into heaven not to honor God but a place where they all could gather to make a name for themselves (Gen. 11:4). God knew that because they were in one accord, there was nothing they could not accomplish together, so he scattered them throughout the land by changing their language. This spread them over the face of the earth (Gen. 11:9).

It wasn't until God called Abraham out of his fatherland of Ur into the promised land of Canaan that a new covenant would be formed (Gen. 12:5). God told Abram or Abraham that if he left his father's land and went into a new land of promise (Canaan), everywhere his feet touched would be his and his descendants' forever. Not only that, but he would multiply his seed as the stars of the sky (Gen. 22:17), which would become the spiritual seed (us, the church) and the sands of the seashore, which represents the Jewish people today or the physical seed of Abraham. A new covenant or fourth dispensation of *promise* for the Jews started out of Abraham. Isaac would be born, then Jacob, who had his name changed to Israel, would have twelve sons who would become the nation of Israel and the twelve tribes that would rule during this time.

We all know the story of how the Jews would eventually be taken captive and held in Egypt as slaves for over four hundred years until Moses would be born to deliver them out of bondage and take them to the promised land (Exod. 12:37-51). Once there, Moses would go up Mt. Sinai, and God would give to him the Ten Commandments or the law by which Israel would now be ruled (Exod. 19:1-24). This began the fifth dispensation of law that would govern the people under the Ten Commandments to show them how hard it was to obey the law and that under law, no man could ever be justified because no man could keep it (Rom. 3:23). The only way God justified the Jews at this time was to have them sacrifice an innocent lamb or goat in the holy of holies on the altar once a year to cover their sins for one more year. This was done in the temple that Solomon had built for the Lord (2 Chron. 5:1-14), later destroyed by Nebuchadnezzar in 606 BC and then once again in 586 BC where the Jews tried to rebel.

It wasn't until Cyrus of the Medo-Persian Empire in 538 BC conquered the Babylonians and authorized the rebuilding of the temple that the walls and the streets were rebuilt, and later in 445 BC, Artaxerxes Longimanus issued the commandment to rebuild the temple (Neh. 2:5). This is the rebuilt temple that Jesus would run the money changers out of one day, all done under the dispensation of law, but that was about to change with the birth of and crucifixion of our

Lord Jesus Christ. He would fulfill the letter of the law and bring in a new dispensation of grace; his shedding of innocent blood on the cross would allow all mankind the chance to enter heaven by accepting and believing in his sacrifice. Even though he died for the whole world, there would still be those who would deny him and his work of the cross and count it as foolishness (1 Cor. 1:18). They would die in their sin (John 8:21), no hope of ever entering into the presence of God, after death then judgment (Hebrew 9:27). All would be cast into hell if they choose to reject his salvation.

For two thousand years, God's grace has been poured out upon mankind. Whosoever wants to be saved and go to heaven just has to ask God for forgiveness of their sins, believe in his only son, Jesus, confess with their mouths, and believe in their hearts that he was raised from the dead (Rom. 10:9-10), and they will be saved—forever! There is no other name given among men by which we can be saved (Acts 4:12). You can try to get to heaven some other way and you will fail. No religion, no cult, no prophet, no man can save (John 1:13) you from the judgment of God. Only the precious blood of Jesus will set you free (John 8:36). Whom the Son sets free is free indeed.

This age will be over shortly. The Rapture of the Church takes place at the end of the age of the Gentiles, which will last seven more years. Then Jesus will come to rule and judge those still on earth to see who will enter the one thousand years of peace in his millennium rule (Matt. 25:32-46). Even though, at the time of his resurrection, Jesus raised paradise and all these Old Testament saints that were in upper Hades (Luke 16:23-24, Matt. 27:52) and took them into heaven, they will not receive their glorified bodies until after the tribulation period so that all those in covenant with God (from Adam on until the last martyr, Jew, or Gentile believer) could be raised up together at the last day of the Gentile rule and the first day of Christ rule (Dan. 12:10-13).

CHAPTER 3

To understand why the Lord will rapture or take his church to heaven before the seven-year tribulation period, he gave us signs that would take place in the last generation living on earth, just before the tribulation would start (Luke 21:28).

In this chapter, I want to share with you some of these signs that are now appearing in our generation that did not appear to any other generation until now, since Jesus was crucified two thousand years ago.

The signs of our time

The first and most important sign and prophecy given to us from the Lord to show us we would be the generation that would not pass away until all these things were fulfilled was that the nation of Israel would come back into their own land from which they had been scattered 2,554 years ago by King Nebuchadnezzar of the old Babylonian Empire. In 1948 on May the fourteenth, Israel became a nation once again in its own land (Ezek. 36:24). Jesus said this generation (born at this time) would not die until he came back (Matt. 24:32), Israel's key to all prophetic revelation of God's time, the line of all fulfillment of God's scriptures. They (the Jews) would be back in their own land before this age closed out and Jesus would return to rule during the millennium reign. There will be two parts to his coming. The first will be in the air (1 Thess. 4:13) when he takes his bride from the earth and takes her to his father's house in heaven (John 14:1-2), where we will stay until the seven years of God's wrath is played out on this earth, called the tribulation period on earth. After these seven years are completed, Jesus with his bride, now his wife (Rev. 19:2-9), will return to earth with us (Rev. 19:14) to judge the earth to see who will be worthy to enter into his one-thousand-year reign (Matt. 25:31-40) and those that are not. The earth will be cleansed of all unbelievers, and only those that are in the "sheep nations"—those that have helped the Jews during this time of trial on earth—will be saved. All believers in Christ will enter into this time of peace and plenty still in their physical bodies (as we presently have). They will continue to populate the earth with thousands upon thousands of new children and families.

So you can see why it's important the Jewish people are established in their own land called Israel and have as their capital the city of Jerusalem.

This sign has now been fulfilled in our generation and has been the center of excitement for all Bible prophecy teachers. This has never been fulfilled in any other generation but ours.

The second sign that God has given us to know we are that chosen generation is when Israel as a nation was put back in their land. In 1948, the city of Jerusalem was not given into their hands. They were given control of the part of Jerusalem but not the old city where the temple mount was, but because of the six-day war in 1967 when Egypt attacked Israel on June 1, 1967, Israel defeated their armies in six days and, on June 6, 1967, took total control of the city of Jerusalem. This city had to be in the control of Israel before (Matt. 24:15) it could be fulfilled in the future where a new temple will be built. This temple will be the temple the Antichrist desolates, called the *Abomination of Desolation*. This temple will be under his control for the last three and a half years of the tribulation period.

The third sign given to this generation living today is the ability to destroy the whole earth in a matter of minutes with nuclear warfare. For over fifty-nine hundred years, man could conquer other nations, but none ever held the destructice power to annihilate the entire planet. Man, with horses and bows and arrows and even guns, up to 1940 could not get the job done, but our generation since 1948 has developed powerful nuclear weapons that we can deliver through any window anywhere around the world in a few minutes. In Revelation 6:8, we see that one-fourth of the world will die of hunger and by "sword," which represents weapons of our day, and in Revelation 9:18, we see one-third of mankind will be killed by fire, smoke, and brimstone. If you add these two together, one-half of all mankind on earth will be killed during the seven years of tribulation. Even if one billion people on earth today are saved and raptured to heaven out of seven billion, this means over three billion people will die during this time. We have the power on earth today to cause this to take place. In 2 Peter 3:10-12, it describes the elements will melt with fervent heat; both the earth and the works in it will be burned up. I don't know about you, but this sounds like nuclear warfare to me. Not only do we here in the USA have the ability to destroy earth, but Russia, China, India, Pakistan, North Korea all have nuclear capabilities to launch their weapons. Iran is in the process of developing these weapons and have already said that they will use them on Israel. God will never allow them to destroy his chosen nation and city, but you can see the time is short and the coming of our Lord is soon. No other generation have ever had these weapons of mass destruction to wipe out all humanity. Jesus himself said that if he had not shortened the time (Matt. 24:22), no flesh would be saved, but because of his elect (those saved during the tribulation period), those days would be shortened.

The fourth sign was the "false Christs" that would rise up in the last generation (Matt. 24:4-5). I think of Jim Jones and the hundreds of people that he took to their deaths in Guyana. He was, at one time, an ordained minister preaching love in God's name, deceiving hundreds into following him into a wilderness away from their loved ones until finally he was the only one who had a Bible and proclaimed he was Christ himself and his word was the only truth. Hundreds believed him and willingly drank the poison that killed them. Others were forced to drink, but it was too late to escape the trap they were in. Today we see preachers proclaiming to represent Christ, but they deny the power therein (2 Tim. 3:5). They are the ones ordaining homosexuals and telling you that everyone will get to heaven because God is a god of love and no one is going to be cast in a burning hell, that this is just a lie of emotional preaching. In 2 Peter 2:1-3, Paul tells us exactly what will happen to these false teachers and preachers who lie to the people about his word—their time of judgment will come (Jude 1:12-13).

God spoke to us about those that say they know God (Rom. 1:21-23) but did not glorify him as God. God gave them up to uncleanness in the lusts of their hearts to dishonor their bodies among themselves (Rom. 1:24-28), women with women and men with men. God gave them over to a debased mind, a mind that actually believes God approves of their actions (Rom. 1:32), but God says that even knowing the righteous judgment of God, those who practice such things are worthy of death. It also said that those who say it's OK to practice these homosexual lifestyles (Rom. 1:32)—the preachers and teachers—are also worthy of death because they approve of these abominations before God (1 Cor. 6:9-10). Don't be deceived, church, these people who practice such things will not enter into heaven. They are not born of the Holy Spirit because they will not put all their sins at the altar. They say God made them like this—they were born homosexual, so there is no repentance needed (1 John 3:7-8). Let no one deceive you; he who practices sin is of the devil, and he who practices righteousness is of God. God loves the sinner but hates the sin; all who come to him in true repentance will be saved and will be born of the Holy Spirit of God (John 3:5). Those that do not will be deceived by Satan, blinded in their minds that all is well (2 Cor. 4:4) and do whatever feels good—it must be OK! They will die in their sins because they believe the lies of the devil, not because God did not love them and do his best to deliver them; they chose the flesh over the belief that God was true and let every man be a liar (Rom. 3:4).

I think of Marshall Applewhite of Heaven's Gate who told his disciples that the Hale-Bopp comet was a spaceship that was coming back for the chosen few. Yes! You guessed it—those that belonged to Heaven's Gate's faith. All they had to do was kill their flesh so their spirits could ascend to the spaceship. So fully dressed, they lay down in bed, took a handful of sleeping pills, put plastic bags over their heads, and suffocated themselves. These were highly intelligent people yet were deceived by a man who claimed to hear directly from these ascended masters or God that they all had to leave on the night the comet passed overhead. This all happened in late March 1997.

Look at Harold Camping, who made predictions the world would end on May 21, 2012, or the Mayan calendar predictions that on December 21, 2012, the world would end.

Now you have national leaders that call themselves Christians out promoting a faith that says Muslims and Christians worship the same God, that there are more ways to God than just Jesus (John 14:6). Paul said that if anyone came preaching any other Christ than the one he preached, let him be accused (2 Cor. 11:4 and verse 13, Gal. 1:8) and for us to look out for ministries that look and act like light but are not! They are actually ministers of Satan. Just because someone has a Bible in their left hand and say they are Christian but their fruit and everything they do in this life is against the Jesus of the Bible, you better know that they are false believers and they are of the devil. They no more have the Holy Spirit in their hearts than I could jump across the Grand Canyon.

I feel sorry for people who come to church without a Bible or believe anything that the preacher says over the pulpit. They have no idea if it really is the Word of God; it sounds spiritual, but Satan himself knows the Word of God and quoted it to Jesus during his temptations in the wilderness (Matt. 4:6, Ps. 91:11-12) about throwing himself off the temple and he would give his angels charge over him—they would bear him up lest he dash his foot against a stone—but Jesus always quoted a scripture, rebuking him.

The road and the way to heaven is narrow, and the road to destruction and hell is wide; many will go the way of death because it is the easy way (Matt. 7:13). The religious leaders of Jesus's time could quote the Old Testament front and back, but they were the deceivers of God's people because they did not know the appearance of their messiah. Even though (Isa. 7:14) God told them a child would be born and his name would be Immanuel (God with us), they killed the Son of God so that they could keep their earthly glory and positions.

Sounds like the politicians of today that have removed God and his Ten Commandments out of government so they can be gods over the people. To keep their little positions of power and control, they are the ones who have agreed to the laws of abortion and murder of innocent babies. They also will pass laws recognizing homosexuality as a normal lifestyle all in the name of "love one another" and "let's all get along." They go out and have their polls that claim most of the people want this, but they are twisters of truth, and they have a judge in heaven that one day will remember *every* thought and every vote they have made to deny him and his Word. God has a record of these people and every person who has ever lived. One day, all will give account (Rev. 20:12).

In this last generation, there will be more deceivers and false Christs (preachers) than have ever been on the earth.

Let's move on to the fifth sign that shows we are the last chosen generation on earth today. This sign is found in Revelation 1:7 and says he is coming with clouds (us), and every eye shall see him. No other generation has ever had the ability to see around the earth except our generation of today. We have satellites circling the globe today so that anyone with a TV can hear and see the news the instant that it takes place. The technology we have today for instant communications is a marvel—miracles unheard of one hundred years ago. E-mailing a message to another person today takes place in a few seconds. When the clouds roll back at the end of the tribulation period and Jesus with his saints comes back to this earth from heaven (Rev. 19:11-14), every eye that has a TV will see him come from heaven to earth. This was not possible in any other generation before ours. Today this prophecy can be fulfilled (Rev. 1:7).

The sixth sign that is unfolding before our eyes today is the developing of a one-world government, a one-world economy, and a one-world religious system. I put all three of these signs as one because all three are taking place as we write these words. John wrote in the book of Revelation, in the thirteenth chapter, that a world leader would arise that would control the world powers; he would be the Antichrist or the Beast (Rev. 13:1) and control the ten kings under his leadership. A second beast would also arise that would be the false prophet or the false religious leader of the religious system that people would embrace after the real church is raptured. All different faiths will come together under the banner of brotherly love so everyone joins together and becomes one. Those that don't will be killed. Their heads will be chopped off.

This is one of the reasons the third part or development of an economy that controls every person on earth takes place (Rev. 13:16-17). After the first three and a half years, the Antichrist is not satisfied just to be the world leader; he wants the people to worship him as God. Satan himself will come into the body of the Antichrist, take control of his mind and body, and set up his satanic kingdom on earth (Rev. 12:12). Today you see the United States and its leaders giving the UN power to take away our rights in this nation; our constitution is being destroyed by leaders under the blinding influence of Satan himself (2 Cor. 4:4).

They claim to know God and (Titus 1:16) his Christ but their fruit reveals them for the false prophets they are. Even our own president claims to know Christ but won't speak at a Christian college (Georgetown) unless they cover up the crosses (1 Cor. 1:18). He gives five-billion-dollar grants to Planned Parenthood so they can continue to murder unborn babies. Do you really think he or anyone else that comes against the true God and denies his will is born of God's spirit? And before you think that I don't have the spiritual authority to judge them, read 1 Corinthians 2:10-16.

If the true believer doesn't bear good fruit but bad fruit (unbeliever), it is cut down and thrown into the fire (Matt. 6:19-20) by the fruit of their lives. You will know them. The greatest deception the world has ever experienced is going on all over the earth today. People are choosing sides now—it's either the New World Order or God's order. Believe his word and in his son, Jesus—there is no other order. One will take you to heaven; the other will take you to hell. You are either of the light (in Christ) or you are blind (in darkness), on your way to serving Satan fully as he takes over the world to control all nations, tongues, and peoples. He must first take away your rights to defend yourself, pass laws to control your right to bear arms. If congress refuses to pass them, then executive orders will be issued from the president that knows best for all of us. Once you have your guns taken and you can't defend your family from an oppressive government, then its "enemies" will begin to disappear, and the "Brown Shirts," like in Hitler's time, will become the private army of the government to help enforce its laws. They can be the IRS or EPA or ACLU or any other form of controlled government agency like Homeland Security that doesn't like what you say against them or their policies. You will be arrested in the beginning, and they will sue you for all your possessions to silence you. If that doesn't work, you will be killed and just disappear in the night.

It's not by accident that our money is being inflated into the trillions of dollars to help destroy the economy. Shortly, around the world, all nations will inflate their money to try to keep up with the purchasing power of the dollar so they can buy the same amount of goods before printing more dollars to buy the same goods. People will begin to realize their money is becoming worthless and try to buy more material things like houses and silver or gold; at this point, money will become worthless, and a new economic system will have to be developed. This brings us to the seventh sign, which is part of the sixth.

The Bible tells us that the Antichrist will set up a *marking system*, which every citizen of the world will have to receive in order to buy or sell anything during the tribulation period (Rev. 13:16-18). No one can buy or sell unless they have this mark on their forehead or in their hands. The Lord told the people with understanding (those that will be born again during the tribulation) to calculate the number of the Beast, 666, and it is a number of a man (Rev. 13:18).

Now to mark or give a number to every person on earth could not have been possible with any other generation before our generation. With the inventors of the computer and its rapid development over the last thirty years wherein we can now go on the Internet and order anything we want around the world. Information is at our fingertips. It will only take the assignment of a "world citizen number" to control what you do on your computer—a number designed with your Social Security number with a world prefix beginning with the number 666 invisibly stamped into your forehead or hand for security reasons. Most people will readily accept this mark as a good thing for it will also show their world leader that they also accept him as God.

PART II
RAPTURE

The Bible tells us in Revelation 14:9-11 that anyone who takes this mark also dooms his soul to hell. He shall be tormented with fire and brimstone in the presence of the Holy Angel and the Lamb forever and ever.

There are today several marking systems that have been developed to bring this to pass. There are microchips the size of a grain of sand that can be inserted under the skin that holds all your business, personal, and medical history in it, and because of satellite technology, you can be traced and found anywhere throughout the world. At some airports, they use a laser eye-recognition machine to check the blood vessels and cornea of your eye to verify who you are. They have developed a radio frequency identification chip that businesses like Walmart use to track all their material purchases. They can track the goods they buy in China from day one, follow it by computer satellite, and know exactly where it is at any given time of movement. When you buy a shirt or pants, this chip will remain in them until they are destroyed. They could, if they wanted to, continue to track those jeans or shirts as long as you have them. Today your cars and trucks can be tracked anywhere in the world—they have computer chips and GPS throughout their systems. Your TVs with the new digital screens and computer chips can listen in and view what you do in your own home. If you think you have a right to your privacy, think again. The government today does not care if you want privacy. They believe they know what is best for you, and they have convinced themselves that they are a lot smarter than you and someone like them needs to think for you and help control your actions so you don't hurt yourself. They are setting up the cameras and listening devices all over every city throughout this nation, telling you it's for your own good to stop the speeding and dangerous drivers on our roads. We have actually believed lies for so long that, like sheep, we just go along until they slaughter us. If you try to raise your voice against them, you are put down as a racist or bigot or someone against the will of the people. If this doesn't shut you up, then the IRS is called to audit you, or you are arrested for being a hater.

This is not happening in someone else's city. It's happening to you in yours. Right before your eyes, you are being enslaved to work and pay taxes that you didn't vote for. Every year they raise taxes on your personal property and every two years on your real estate without a vote of the people. You work all your life, thinking that someday you'll retire, own your home and go fishing, maybe even take that vacation you and your wife dreamed about. Then when you finally retire and your health begins to fail, any money you saved is eaten up by medical bills and inflation because we have a government that prints bogus bills to inflate the economy and destroy the value of the hard-earned dollars you worked for, for over thirty years. They keep raising taxes without representatives of the people until you have to sell the property you bought thirty years ago to retire in and live a happy, peaceful life in your old age. You now have to move to a substandard, low-income neighborhood in order to live out your life. Social security that you paid into all your working life is now different because your trusty government took your money out of it, replaced it with IOUs, and spent it to grow more government so more of their buddies could have good incomes paid for from your SS retirement account. Both Republicans and Democrats did that to you. They are both out to steal your money and freedom.

One acts like the good guy, and the other, the bad guy. Then they reverse the scene, depending on the political winds at the time. But each one's policies are pushed through, and no one really takes the blame, and the people (sheep) vote them back in, thinking they did their best. Let me give it to you straight. They are taking away your freedom slowly and giving them to the United Nations to develop a one-world government. They want to control your every move and set up a digital credit system in our economy so that no product will be sold or bought without a tracking or marking system wherein they will be able to charge and collect a world sales tax. Every world citizen will have to pay this tax to breathe and eat. There will be a national ID card issued in the near future. This will also act as your passport. Without it, you will not be able to fly out of the country or conduct business in any other nation. Money will be a thing of the past. This universal ID card will also act as a credit card. It will be accepted everywhere around the world. When you buy something, it will be electronically deducted from your account or credited if you sell something or earn credits or dollars from your employment.

This may sound a little like *Star Wars* to some, but the Bible tells us that it is coming in Revelation 13, and it has proved to be 100 percent correct in my reading and study of scriptures now for over thirty years. You make your own decisions in its veracity and truth to your own peril. All have to make their own conclusions to God's truth (Rom. 3:4), but God says, "Let him be true and every man a liar."

We, today, are living in a world that believes they (the leaders) are the chosen few that will lead the peoples of the nations to gather together in peace and brotherhood and everyone will live together in harmony and safety. No more wars and poverty—everyone will share alike, and there will be no more fighting and death.

All they have to do is get rid of all these religious people that believe there is only one way to heaven. They must shut up preachers that preach that Jesus Christ is the only way to God (John 14:6), that all other teachings or religions will not get you to God, that no other name given to man under heaven will get you there other than the name of Jesus (Acts 4:12). They must begin to destroy the foundation of the faith.

The first thing they did was to take prayer out of schools in 1962 so the children wouldn't have a basis of belief every day to talk to God. The next year, in 1963, they took the Ten Commandments from the schools. Now children would be educated with no moral values or guidelines like "Thou shall not kill (or lie)." To go further, in 1973, *Roe v. Wade* allowed women to kill their little babies before they were born. Now life was beginning to have little value in the mind of young adults, having grown up believing in no God and no moral values. They were taught they had come from scum in the water, that monkeys were their distant cousins—they had just evolved over a period of billions of years and had no value other than "the strong will survive." Today the government has convinced the people that the constitution says that there is a separation of state and religion. Nowhere in our constitution does it ever say that. It says that the government cannot make any laws prohibiting the free expression of our religion, not that religion was not to be part of government. Most or all our leaders back then had a belief or respect of the almighty God and his commandments and values.

Today you see presidents with a Bible in their left hand, telling you how they love God while they pass abortion bills and promote abominable sins like homosexual lifestyles in opposition to God's Word (1 Cor. 6:9-20). God help them because they will not escape his judgment or anyone else who agrees with them. We now have generations of families who do not know God or his son, Jesus, today. They have children that are now going into the schools they grew up in and killing and murdering innocent children just for the fun of it. Why not? They are just some things that aren't worth anything; they came from pond scum. They will just die and cease to exist. There is no God, no judgment; live your life the way you want to. Enjoy the flesh, sex, drugs, alcohol; tomorrow you die, then it's over—no more worries. The Bible says it's been appointed unto man once to die then the judgment (Heb. 9:27).

Look at this eighth sign, the prophecy in Revelation 9:16 where a two-hundred-million-man war army will march across the earth and kill one-third of mankind (Rev. 9:18). During the time of John the apostle, there were not throughout the known world at that time a hundred million people. For this prophecy to come to pass, it could only take place in a generation where a nation could muster up this number of men. Do you know that today, in 2013, there are three different nations or groups of people that can produce an army of that size? First, we have the Chinese that have 1.6 billion people that boasted in the past that they could raise an army of two hundred million. They spoke this very number of two hundred million men and fulfilled John's prophecy in the ninth chapter of Revelation. I believe this will be the last army in Revelation 16:12-16 that will be gathered in the Valley of Armageddon to face God's judgment with the Antichrist and false prophet. The second nation that has the ability to march forth this big an army is India. They have 1.4 billion people, and they are well able to call them to the front lines. India is also a nuclear power and could do extreme damages to the world—one-third of the world's population left on earth during the tribulation period. There will be around three billion people killed, almost 10 times the entire population of the United States.

The third nation or nations of the Middle East are the Muslim groups. Together they have around 1.2 billion Muslims that could form a two-hundred-million-man army to try to destroy Israel and anyone else who disagrees with their faith. The president of Iran had obviously fulfilled the prophecy in Psalms 83:4 when he made the statement to wipe Israel off the map and cut them off from being a nation so the name of Israel may be remembered no more. Well, I have news for Mr. Abinaijib—when he is no more, Israel and the Jewish people will still be on the earth.

There are three ways the nations of today can now bring forth this massive army. Not before our generations was this possible, but it can now happen tomorrow.

The ninth sign I want to share with you was prophesied seven hundred years before Jesus came to be birthed in the earth. It's found in Ezekiel 38:1-5. It's a prophecy about a nation, Magog, to the far north of Israel, which we recognize as Russia today, and Gog, its leader. This land was where the Scythians settled north and northeast of the Black Sea and east of the Arab Sea, where it's now occupied by Russia. Rosh, Meshech, and Tubal are in the area of modern-day Turkey. The other allies of Russia will be Persia or Iran/Iraq. Ethiopia is today's northern Sudan. Libya and Gomar, the eastern part of Turkey, and the Ukraine and the House of Togarmah near the Syrian border (Ezek. 38:5-6).

The reason this prophecy is an important sign for our generation is that God will bring these nations up against Israel to destroy 5/6 of their armies (Ezek 39:2) and also the Muslim nations that align themselves with Russia (Ezek. 38:8-9). Two thousand six hundred years ago, there were no Russians or even Muslims to come against Israel. Russia was not ever a powerful nation until after World War II and into the early 1950s. The Muslim nations did not have any major treaties with Russia until recently. Now Iran and Syria have signed oil treaties with Russia in exchange for their military protection into the year 2035. China has also began to do business with Russia, and they have became buddy-buddy. What we see developing in our generation is a distancing relationship between the United States of America and Russia, China, Iran, and the Muslim nations growing closer together against the nations of Israel.

Ezekiel says that Russia will one day think on evil thoughts, and these nations will attack Israel (Ezek. 38:16), but they all will be destroyed by God himself around the mountaintops of Israel (Ezek. 38:21-22). He will leave one-fifth of them so that all nations will know that he is God. Russia will attack Israel because they want to control the oil in the Middle East. The Muslims just want to annihilate every Jew on the face of the earth, but they will be the ones caught in their own trap. As we see world events unfolding, Russia and these Muslim nations will now align themselves against Israel and any nation that attacks them. I believe Israel very soon will bomb Iran's nuclear facilities to slow down their efforts to create a nuclear device or bomb capable of destroying Jerusalem or one of their major cities. When this happens, Iran will call on the "Russia agreement" to protect them against all enemies that would attack them. Russia will be drawn into the Middle East like a fish with a hook in its mouth. They really won't want to go, but the treaties they signed will force them to commit to defend Iran. I also think a thought will come into their heads—that this is the right time (Ezek. 38:10) to take control of the entire Middle East (including Iran) and control the oil and riches by becoming the strong military power there and take over by forcing all the nations that would resist. The surprise will come when no nation around the world comes to Israel's aid—they will be totally cut off from all hope—but then their God from heaven, Jehovah, will step into the battle and fight for his people, the Jews, and destroy these armies around the mountains of

Israel, destroying them and their nations from ever becoming much of a threat in the future (Ezek. 38:18-22).

Some believers believe this is World War III. It's not much of a world war! These nations will attack Israel, and God will destroy them in a short space of time. He will declare that their destruction is for his glory, that now the whole world will know his name (Ezek. 38:23).

With Russia, Iran, Iraq, and the other Middle Eastern nations out of the picture, there will now be a need for a leader to rise up out of the European countries to fill the void. I believe the Antichrist will rise up at this time with the answers to world peace. With the threat of Muslim domination now gone, he will enter into a seven-year peace treaty with Israel (Dan. 9:26-27) and allow them to rebuild their temple right beside the Muslims' Dome of the Rock of Omar. This will allow all religions to exist peacefully side by side. The Jewish people will go back to animal sacrifices for the first three and a half years into this treaty, but then the Antichrist will break his covenant with Israel, enter into their temple, set up the abomination of desolation (Matt. 24:15, Dan. 9:27), and set up a image of himself to be worshipped as God.

Now that he has control of the world economic system, he will require a marking system to be implemented by placing a biochip or bar code in or on everyone in the world who wants to buy or sell (Rev. 13:16). No one can get food or gas or any houses, vehicles, and clothes without first taking the mark. The Bible is very clear that if anyone receives this mark, they doom their souls to an eternal hell (Rev. 14:9-10). The hardest thing for a father or mother is to see their family without food. It will be extremely hard to live and eat under the radar of the Antichrist at this time. It can be done and will be done because there will be people that will help—God calls them sheep nations (Matt. 25:34-40)—they will help those escape the hand of the Antichrist. If caught and if they refuse the mark, which will also be an acceptance of the Antichrist as God, they will be beheaded for their faith, but they will go to heaven and spend eternity with God Almighty. The tribulation period will not be a pleasant time to be on earth. Once again, over one-half of the population of the world will die. God has given to us his grace through his son, Jesus, to escape all these things if we will but accept him as our personal savior (Luke 21:36).

If you have not yet invited Jesus to forgive you of your sins, do so now. Get on your knees and ask for his forgiveness. Believe in your heart that he died for your sins and gave his life for yours, that through his death, burial, and resurrection, you can have new life in him (Rom. 10:9-10). Confess with your mouth, and believe in your heart, and God will forgive you and accept you into his family of God. By saying this simple prayer, you are now a child of God and belong to him. You are washed in his blood and born of his incorruptible seed (1 Pet. 1:18-23). Now through your faith in him, renew your mind to his Word so that you will know the good, acceptable, and perfect will of God for your life (Rom. 12:2-3).

Just going to a church will not renew your mind to God's Word. You must read and study to show yourself approved by God (2 Tim. 3:16-17). Spend time every day in prayer and study of the Word. Get it down into your memory, and begin to quote it to yourself. Claim the promise in it for you and your family. Your life will begin to change for the best as God hears your prayers for your future. He has come to give you an abundant life (John 10:10) and to prosper your family.

There is one more sign that I would like to share with you in this chapter. It is the tenth sign that Jesus said would be on the earth before his return, and it's found in Luke 17:28. Jesus said it would be like the days of Sodom and Gomorrah. People would be eating and drinking, buying and selling; they would build houses and plant fields. They also were a morally bankrupt society. Their judges and city officials allowed for anything that goes. They voted in homosexuality and set up laws to protect them. They could even walk the streets in gangs and have sex with whomever they chose. There was no fear of prosecution or going to jail. Their city leaders were on their side; they would just make another law, and everything would be legal (Gen. 19:1-11). When the two angels entered Sodom to talk with Lot, they were going to stay in the square overnight, but Lot (verse 3) insisted strongly for them to stay in his house. The homo gang, both young and old members, still came to Lot's house to forcefully drag them out of his home to have physical (carnal) sex with them. He went outside to talk with them and offered his two virgin daughters to them if they would leave these men alone. In verse 8, Lot also makes the statement that it was for this very reason of their evil act of homosexuality that these men had come to his house.

We know from verse 9 that when they mocked Lot about being a judge. They were in control of the city and would deal worse with him at a later time. They pressed hard against Lot, trying to break down his door. The angels pulled Lot back into the house and struck the people with blindness so that they were not able to find the door. The reason God destroyed Sodom and Gomorrah was because of the sin of perversion—homosexuality (Gen. 19:13). The outcry of their sin was great before the face of the Lord. Today, nothing has changed. Homosexuality is still an abomination against God (Lev. 20:13). No matter how many judges, city officials, presidents, senators, or representatives change the law, when we sit back and accept what these immoral people in office promote (all in the name of the so-called people they represent), we all become part of the destruction of our nation and cities. Once this sin is promoted as a natural lifestyle, then all other forms of sexual immorality will also become OK—pornography, pedophilia, cross-dressing. transsexuality—if one is OK, they are all OK.

The same thing happened in Sodom, and we now have Barney Frank and many others in government positions to vote in the hate laws and uphold the evil in our nation. Everyone who votes for these people will also share in their sins (Rom. 1:32).

When we prefer to be wiser than God, he calls us fools and begins to let us believe the lie (Rom. 1:21-23). If you believe that it's OK for men to have sex with men and women to have sex with women, that God is a God of love and that he wants us to be happy and live with whomever we want as a partner (and besides, God made them like that, so let's just accept their lifestyle and let them live their life the way they want to), you, my friend, have just embraced the lie that will bring you into the same judgment as them.

God loves all people. All of us are sinners, and some of us were involved with this sin before we were saved or delivered from it (1 Cor. 6:9-11), but make no mistake; those that love their sin more than the truth of Christ (John 3:17-21) and those that help promote it or agree to it will all face a judgment of condemnation. They will not inherit the kingdom of God. Today, just before Jesus comes back to this earth, he said these conditions would exist, and we see it all taking place right before our eyes. Yes! I am sorry to say, but the elected officials and the appointed judges are already in place, and legalized homosexual marriages are in place. Laws will be put on the books to keep preachers from preaching out against this evil, awful sin of perversion. Your children, if in public schools, will be corrupted with the teaching that this is a natural lifestyle, that two mommies or two daddies are OK. We have reached a point in the United States where evil is called good (Isa 5:20) and anyone who stands up for good is called evil, a bigot, or uncompromising. We have leaders that are in the highest offices of the land; they are liars and unworthy of our votes. But even after they are found out, the people vote them in again so they can receive checks that they promise to give them out of the workingman's pocket. People have sold out their birthright and have chosen to align themselves with the devil of the Bible.

They have taken prayer and the Ten Commandments out of our schools and wonder why killings are taking place in our schools. We have a generation of kids that do not know it's wrong to kill. They play all day with Hollywood video games that kill a person every second. Their minds have become so warped they do not know right from wrong. Most marriages end in divorces around the 50 percent range. Children are raised by one parent who has to work all day and very seldom has much social time with them. Many are raised by drug users that don't want anything to do with them. They go to the streets where gangs become their family. They have kids who grow up the same way. There is no wall of morality to guide them. The Ten Commandments of God were what our nations' laws were built upon; they kept us in line with what is right and what is wrong. Now laws are put in the books and interpreted by judges that do what they think is right to do. We have a president that has sworn to uphold the laws of our constitution and nation but will not enforce the laws of immigration. These are impeachable offenses but no one has impeached him. Why? It's because both parties, Republican and Democrat, want the same goal and that is to enslave the people to a one-world government and control them. It's not coming to the USA; it is already here, as quickly as they can destroy your constitution and get you to accept it. Then you, one day, will wake up under their control and be enslaved. Your rights of free speech and the right to protect yourself will be turned over to the one-world government—they will be gone. One day, they also will come for you.

I have given you ten signs that are happening in our generation, and I have ten more I could share, backed up by scriptures, but I will save them for a later time. The odds of our generation being the generation that can fulfill all these prophecies mathematically is astronomical. God is telling us we are that generation of peoples that will see the coming of the Lord. For us, first, his church, then after seven years in heaven, we will come back with him to the earth, and we will forever be with him.

CHAPTER 4

To understand how all these prophecies affect us today and what we need to continue to look for as the day of the Lord draws near is to bring into a simple focus the picture of the world settings of nations and how their positioning influences world events and how they fulfill prophecy. Instead of dealing with every little nation on earth, let's break the world down by superpowers and how they influence the world today.

The United States of America is, by far, the major superpower of the world. We control the most powerful military on earth today. There is no question of who we are and what we can control with the weapons we have. Our ability to destroy the world with nuclear weapons is without doubt. We also have control of the world's economic system because we have the reserve currency that is used to measure the weight or value of all nations' currency. For example, if a country inflates its dollars by printing more in their nation (like doubling their dollars) and if before the printing, it took one US dollar to equal one dollar of their money (it was an equal purchasing power). If they double their money by printing more of their currency, it becomes two of their dollars for one of ours because they have inflated their value. This system has worked properly and worked for all nations of the world until now, in our generation. The status of the United States as its only real superpower is now threatened because of the leadership we have put in high offices. These leaders have printed trillions of dollars, of "fiat dollars," to pay for programs and to expand government rule that we can't pay back. We now have over seventeen trillion dollars of debt, and it's expected to be twenty-two trillion by the year 2020. This has eroded the purchasing power of all your dollars since 2007. What are your dollars worth today in 2013? Nothing—not even the cost of the paper they are written on. They are backed by nothing but the Federal Reserve Corp—that is not even a government-controlled bank. They are a private corporation that is controlled by private investors. They can print as many dollars as they want.

When people wake up and realize that trillions of worthless dollars are floating around, everyone seems to have plenty of them. Prices begin to rise. A gallon of milk that used to be $1.69 in 2007 is now $3.69 in 2013. A gallon of gas, $1.89 in 2008, is now $3.50. People see prices rising; they begin to realize their money that they have saved for twenty years is losing its purchasing power. They begin to buy real property like houses, gold, or silver, then prices rise faster until it takes one million dollars to buy a car. This is how a superpower becomes a second-rate nation. Now you may be thinking that this may be true, but we still have military superiority.

That is true today, but not for long. We have a president in control of the White House that is systematically disarming our nuclear arsenal by reducing our missile systems and missiles to bring them from over ten thousand warheads to three hundred. We will not be able to defend if several conflicts happen at once.

The states of the United States are rapidly being destroyed within, and it won't be much longer before any nation can challenge us and we will not respond.

The second military power on earth today is Russia; they have a nuclear might of somewhere around twelve thousand to fourteen thousand missiles. No one really knows—they may have twice this amount. I don't believe any of these nations are truthful when it comes to their nuclear-missile might. When the Berlin Wall came down in the late '80s peace and safety throughout the world became possible. Because the Cold War that existed between the United States and Russia could now be mended, all of us could be friends and relax about a nuclear war breaking out. But Russia has been building its nuclear armament since then, and we have been reducing ours, believing one day, the whole world will disarm.

The only way a nation can truly have peace in this age is through a strong defense. If they know you can and will destroy them if they attack you, they will not commit self-destruction.

The third military power we have on earth today is China. They not only have plenty of nuclear weapons but they also have, I believe, the largest standing army in the world today. With 1.6 million people, they can muster a two-hundred-million-man army with no problems. The Bible declares that the people of the East will do just that (Rev. 9:16, Rev. 16:13-16). China will play a major role in the end times at the battle of Armageddon; we will bring all the nations into focus, and the part they all will play in the last seven years on earth will be called the tribulation period.

The fourth major power on earth with nuclear weapons and a standing army is Israel today. Make no mistake—they can and will defend their nation if they have to. We know God will defend them, and they will never be destroyed or removed from the earth. This is the nation that all prophecy surrounds itself about. When any nation comes against Israel, they will be broken and defeated (Zech. 12:3). God made this nation of people to be his. Anyone who comes against it will be cut to pieces. Those that believe God has forsaken the Jewish people have not read their Bible (Rom. 11:1-5). The Lord will bring his people back into the vine of life, back to himself, their messiah, during the tribulation period. More on this later.

The fifth major power is the country of India. They also have nuclear weapons and have about 1.4 billion people that have the ability to put together a two-hundred-million-man army.

I have already mentioned these numbers and nations earlier, but now we will try to show you how they fit in prophecy in these last days.

The sixth power is the European common-market countries; they have come out of the old Roman Empire, and out of one of these countries, the Antichrist will come. There are over twenty-five countries that make up this union, but during the rule of the Antichrist, there will only be ten nations in which he will rise up out of and control (Dan. 7:7-8, Rev. 13:1, Rev. 17:12). There could be thirteen nations because he plucks three out by war, but only ten nations will rule with him (Dan. 7:8-9).

These nations will be the main players during the final seven years of Gentile rule on earth. There are other nations like Pakistan, Great Britain, and others that play a minor role, but now let us look at how all these pieces fit together in the lead up to the beginning of the tribulation period and the parts these nations play during the seven years with the Antichrist.

One of the reasons the catching-away or Rapture of the Church is so important is the disappearance of millions of people. It will take place before the Antichrist can be revealed (2 Thess. 2:3).

There will be a tremendous void of people throughout the world. Different nations will be affected, depending on the number of Christians in each of these nations. I believe the United States will be affected the most. If over 50 percent of citizens are truly born again of the spirit of God in America, it will devastate the economy of the United States. Many military leaders and government officials will be gone along with most of the working people. We will have no one left to pay mortgages to banks or taxes to city, state, or federal government; it will collapse the system we are now governed by. But in Russia, they have less than three million people in the underground church, and their government won't even miss them, probably won't even know they're gone nor will they care. The same thing will happen in China. The church is underground for fear of persecution and arrest. Or in Hindu and Muslim nations—to them, the Christians they have in their nations are troublemakers, always teaching love and that Jesus is the Son of God and the only way to heaven. I hope you are beginning to see that the Rapture of the Church will change the world we are now living in, and all nations will have to rethink their positions and status in the power structure of this world.

There will be three major wars during this time of tribulation and several small conflicts that the Antichrist will battle with to achieve world power (Dan. 11:36-40). The major wars will be (1) World War III

(Ezek. 38:1-5), (2) the battle for Israel, when the Antichrist sets himself up as God (Matt. 24:15, Dan. 9:27) and breaks his covenant with them.

The third and final battle will be the battle of Armageddon where the Antichrist's forces and the two-hundred-million-man army of the east and all other nations that join them against Christ will gather in the Valley of Jezereel, where Christ will come back with his saints and destroy them at the end of the last day of tribulation in the valley when the blood will run to the horses' bridles (Rev. 19:11-18).

But why do all these nations react the way they do, and how do all these parts (nations) fit together in the last days?

No one but God knows the exact way it all comes about, but he has given us enough insight into his Word to help us see through the glass more than just darkly. There are a lot of good prophecy teachers in our day to help us look at different outcomes that will take place during this period. You must allow the Holy Spirit to show you all truth in any revelations. Only he can reveal to you his Word and how it builds your faith in what is to come.

We know today that the world is on course to implode. How long it will take to play itself out is anyone's guess—it could be two years or thirty years from now. But you can be sure of one thing—it will happen; God has declared it to be so!

But what if I were to tell you God has given us a way to see into the future if the Rapture of the Church was to happen in our generation? First, realize that no one knows the day or hour that Jesus will return (Matt. 24:36). But we are to be aware of the signs of the times (1 Thess. 5:1-11). We are not to be caught unaware. Most would agree with me that the earthquakes, famines, floods, wars, and rumors of wars, the strange weather patterns, and the falling away from God's son and his Word are upon us.

So if the disappearance of millions of people took place today, how would the world react? What would the picture look like around the world? The United States as a world superpower would be decimated without people to serve its government and business. A loss of 50 percent to 60 percent of its population would make all its military might ineffective—not enough leaders to direct its movements. The confusion it causes throughout this nation will take months and maybe years to bring back on line.

But what about Russia? It will have lost less than three or four million people, and they will hardly be missed. Its military might will still be in place with hardly any disruption, and I believe they will see this as an opportunity for gain.

As we know today, Israel is surrounded by enemies that want to destroy them, especially Iran and its president. They are trying to develop nuclear warheads to place on missiles to annihilate the country of Israel and wipe them off the map (Ps. 83:4). What if Israel were to bomb their nuclear development centers to slow down their plans to destroy them. According to today's signed agreements between Russia and Iran, if attacked, they are to help protect or defend Iran up to the year 2035 in exchange for oil from Iran.

This would pull Russia into the war against Israel even if they didn't want to go. But the Bible says that Magog (Russia) and its leader, Gog, think an evil thought (Ezek. 38:10).

When the Rapture takes place, Russia will see its opportunity to take control of all the resources in the Middle East and become the superpower they have always wanted to be. Iran and their cronies will become pawns to be used to attain their goals and then become slaves to their will.

But are they in for a surprise because we know that God is going to destroy five-sixth of them around about the mountaintops of Israel and only leave one-sixth of them to tell the story so that God gets the glory. This will be World War III, but it will not last very long. By the time the rest of the world tries to decide what to do, this war will be over (Ezek. 38:1-23, Ezek. 39:1-12). Israel will bury the bodies for seven months and their weapons for seven years. This war is different from the battle that will take place at the end of the seven years of tribulation called Armageddon.

This battle takes place around the mountains of Israel. Armageddon is in the valley of Megiddo. Russia clearly is named (Ezek. 39:2) as the county of the far north and the kings of the East at Armageddon (Rev. 16:12). This battle takes place right after the Rapture for a reason. The

United States and now Russia will no longer be threats as superpowers to control the world. The next power still left to take advantage of this void will be the old Roman Empire or the European common-market countries. The Antichrist will come out of one of these countries as a man of peace, and he will have the answers to the world economic problem and stability in the world. He will rise to power quickly and become the one that will sign a seven-year peace treaty with Israel. I'm not sure, but he may even take credit for the defeat of Russia and the Muslim nations, proclaiming that now it's time for peace in the world, time for Israel to rebuild their temple and be at peace side by side with their Arab brothers, time for the world to disarm and begin to plant and grow food to stop world hunger, to set up a world system of government and economics, a new-world religious system where everyone gets along headed by a religious leader the Bible calls the false prophet (Rev. 13:11-13).

This all works great for the first three and a half years while the Antichrist is building his base of power with ten other leaders he has appointed to control the earth (Rev. 17:12). Israel is resting in peace, and once again, the temple is rebuilt and they are offering animal sacrifice for *their* sins. But the Antichrist is not satisfied with just power to rule over the whole earth. He wants to be God and worshipped as God. Since Satan has now been cast to the earth (Rev. 12:9-13, Dan. 12:1), he knows he has but a short time (the last three and a half years). He possesses the Antichrist and breaks his seven-year covenant with Israel in the middle of it (Matt. 24:15, Dan. 9:2) and sets himself up as God.

This is the second war in which the Antichrist will try to take control of Israel. One-third of Israel will flee the city and go into the country of Jordan—into Moab-Amon and Edom where the city of Petra is—and stay there for three and a half years (Zech. 13:7-9). Two-thirds of Israel will be cut off or killed, but God will save a remnant. In order for the world to bow down and worship the Antichrist as God, the devil will set up a marking system through the false prophet so that every citizen in the world that wants to buy or sell anything must take a mark in their forehead or right hand (Rev. 13:16). If they don't, they will be killed or beheaded.

Now this brings up the reason the Third World War will start and end at the battle of Armageddon. China has been patient and has pretty much left the Roman leader alone to take the lead in the world. They really didn't say much when he stood up and took the reins of leadership and proclaimed a peace treaty with Israel and even took credit for Russia's defeat.

He had answers for the world's hunger problem, and there seemed to be an order of peace. But now he had stepped over the line. He wanted everyone to call him God and bow down by taking his mark, and the Chinese were not about to call him master.

So they called forth their standing army of two hundred million soldiers and marched to the Middle East to conquer him and his armies and to take control of the entire world. If there were any other gods, then when they got there, they would defeat them also. In the book of Joel (Joel 2:1-11), this army will march across the lands toward Israel, and everything in their path would be destroyed. A fire will devour before them and a flame behind them. By the time these kings of the East get to Israel and gather at the Valley of Jezereel, nothing will escape them, but they will be drawn to this valley, and they with their armies and the nations of the world plus the Antichrist's armies will all meet Jesus here and be destroyed at this last battle called Armageddon (Zech. 14:3-5). The Lord will come and all his saints with him. This will end the reign of the Antichrist and the false prophet. Both of them will be cast into the Lake of Fire (Rev. 19:20). Satan will be thrown in the bottomless pit for one thousand years (Rev. 20:2). Jesus will judge the nations at the end of the tribulation period, and we will all enter into the millennium of peace for one thousand years (Matt. 25:34-46).

I believe the Rapture of the Church can happen at any time. Nothing else needs to be fulfilled before Jesus comes back for his bride and the tribulation period begins.

2 Peter 3:9

Today we see all these nations lining up and being put in place like chess pieces on a board; they are now positioned around the world, ready to play out their roles. According to God's final act in this end-time scenario of the separation of those that will spend eternity with him or those that will spend an eternity without him, God loves the entire world and doesn't (2 Pet. 3:9) want anyone to perish, but man has chosen to deny the God of the Bible and has forsaken the way of salvation. But make no mistake—God's plan will unfold just like he has said in his scriptures. We (prophecy teachers) may not have it all in the right place as it takes place, but it will happen! Just as God has declared it. No one who is born of God's spirit should ever worry about going through the terrible time of tribulation. God loves you with his whole being and will not hurt you in any way. The purpose of this age of grace is to take out a bride for his son, and nothing is going to stop that from happening, and God is well able to protect and keep us from harm until he comes back and takes us out of here (John 10:27-30). Once again, God's wrath is reserved for those sons of disobedience (Eph. 2:2), not for us who are obedient to receive his son as our savior (Rom. 5:9, 1 Thess. 5:9).

We are at peace with God, and he has poured his love into our hearts (Rom. 5:1-5). We don't have to war any longer with God; he is our father, and we are his children (1 John 3:1-2).

We have shared with you how we believe the nations will react once the Rapture of the Church takes place. Now I want to share with you reasons why the rapture or the catching-away of the body of Christ must take place.

The first reason we will be taken from the earth before the tribulation period is because the bride must be taken into heaven to be in the Father's house (John 14:1-4).

Jesus gave us a promise that when he was here, he would come again and receive us to himself and that where he was, we would be also. He wants his bride to be with him in heaven, so he can proudly show her off to the entire kingdom of God. The father had chosen her before the foundation of the world began (Eph. 1:3-4). He had already declared to his entire creation of beings that serve him that she would be the one his son would die for and be with him for eternity in love and be holy before him.

The second reason is that the Lord did not give us a *spirit of fear* (2 Tim. 1:7). But the scriptures tell us that in this time of tribulation, men's hearts will be failing them because of the things coming upon the earth (Luke 21:25-26). There will be great fear upon the earth as God begins to pour his judgments out on the earth. God said he would keep his bride from the hour of trial that would come upon the earth to try the whole earth (Rev. 3:10).

So many Christians today want to believe and teach that God's children will go through the tribulation period, whether for the first three and a half years (midtribulation) or the whole seven years (posttribulation) before God raptures them and takes them to heaven. This is to deny the many wonderful promises in God's Word to keep us safe. It is Christ who said to pray always that you may be counted worthy to escape all these things that will come to pass upon the earth (Luke 21:36). My friends, don't you think you are worthy the moment you asked Jesus to forgive you of your sins and you believed in his work on the cross, accepted his forgiveness, and invited him into your heart? Don't live your life in fear any longer. You don't have to buy a cave somewhere and hide out or store food so you can survive the tribulation time. God is coming back for you to take you home. This brings up the third important reason God has to take you out of the world before he can pour his wrath out on it. In the book John 3:36, he wrote that he that believes in the Son has everlasting life, and he who does not have the Son shall not see life but the wrath of God abides in him. But for the believer, in 1 Thessalonians 1:10, it tells us to wait for his son from heaven who will deliver us from the wrath to come. One (the unbeliever) will receive wrath, but the other (the believer) will not. This is not hard to comprehend. God did not appoint us to his wrath (1 Thess. 5:9) but to obtain deliverance or salvation. He said much more than that—having now been justified by his blood, we shall be saved from wrath through him (Rom. 5:9).

God did not give you a spirit of fear but of power and a sound mind (2 Tim. 1:7). Your mind would not be very sound if God poured his wrath out upon you.

The fourth reason the church must be taken out of here is so God can go back to dealing with the Jewish people. There is still one week or seven years of judgment that they will have to go through. The church today has been given the great commission of preaching the gospel or good news to every creature around the world (Matt. 28:18). Today whosoever can come (John 3:16) to Jesus and be saved, and the gates of hell cannot prevail against the church (Matt. 16:18). Once the church is gone (raptured), God will seal 144,000 Jewish evangelists (Rev. 7:4), twelve thousand out of every tribe, and they will begin to preach that the Messiah is coming. They will receive the revelation of Christ as I believe Saul, or Paul, received on the way to Damascus through a blinding light experience (Acts 9:3-17). They will be the preachers for the first three and a half years of tribulation, and then I believe the two witnesses will finish the last three and a half years and be killed by the Antichrist in the last four days before Christ returns to earth with his saints (Rev. 11:3-12).

More on this subject later. But remember what I said about the gates of hell not prevailing against the church. As long as the church is on earth, we will always be able to overcome and defeat the devil (Luke 10:19). All power has been given to the church to overcome him, but did you notice that in the tribulation period he has been given the authority to overcome the tribulation saints? Revelation 13:7 says, "The church is gone from the earth," and God deals with his Jewish people to come back to the Messiah (Jesus), and the greatest revival the world has ever seen takes place (Rev. 7:14). God's wrath is poured out upon the world, and Satan will be able to overcome the saints. We cannot be on earth when this happens.

The fifth reason God will take us from the earth to heaven is so that the entire Body of Christ can be one together. Half of the Body of Christ today is in heaven, either by natural death or among those that have been slain for the Word of God and their testimony of Jesus. The rest of his body is still on earth, waiting for him to come for us, and he will! In Ephesians 1:10, he tells us that in the dispensation of the fullness of the times, he might gather together in one (all things in Christ) his *church*, which are both in heaven and on earth in him. In Ephesians

1:9, he said he had made known to us the mystery of his will, that it was because of his good pleasure, purposed in himself, that he was coming back with the body in heaven to unite with the rest of his body on earth. Jesus is coming back for you and me! And in a twinkling of an eye, the trumpet will sound, the dead in Christ (those coming back with Jesus) will be raised, and then we who are alive on earth shall be changed and rise to be with the Lord forever (1 Cor. 15:51-52, 1 Thess. 4:13-18).

Therefore, comfort one another with these words. There would not be much comfort in his word if we had to live through his wrath.

The sixth reason we will be in heaven is to see our Lord and Savior crowned King of Kings and Lord of Lords. In Revelation 5:4-6, John begins to weep (in verse 4) because no one was found worthy throughout the entire kingdom of God to receive and open the scroll to look at it. But one of the elders (of the church) told him not to weep; the lion of the tribe Judah had prevailed to open and loose its seven seals. Verse 6 says in the midst of the elders or the church, his body, stood a lamb as though it was slain having seven horns (all power), seven eyes (all knowing), and seven spirits (total fullness). He was able to take the scroll from the right hand of God the Father. We will all be there as Jesus takes control of the title deed of the earth. He paid for its rights back to God, his father, when he died on the cross of Calvary, shed his blood, and gave his life so we could live. But now he takes control with us safely in heaven with him; he will now release the seals that have been held in reserve for the time of God's wrath to be released (Rev. 6:1).

This brings up the seventh reason we will be in heaven before God can release his wrath, and it's found in 2 Thessalonians 2:2-3. Paul said in verse 2 not to be soon shaken in mind or spirit or troubled either by spirit or by word or letter that the day of the Lord had come. Let no one deceive you by *any* means, for that day will not come unless the falling away (apostasy) comes first and the man of sin is revealed, the Son of Perdition or the Antichrist, is revealed. He opposes God and exalts himself above "all that is called God's," and even sets himself up as God in the temple of God in the last three and a half years of tribulation (Matt. 24:15, Rev. 13:8). The Bible says in 2 Thessalonians 2:7 that he who now restrains the Holy Spirit will do so until he is taken out of the way, and only then can the lawless one be revealed (Antichrist). The word *apostasy* in Greek means more than just "falling away"; it also means "divorce" or "departure."

Paul is telling the Thessalonians to not be afraid concerning our gathering together with the Lord (1 Thess. 2:1), that until the church is gone (taken out by the Holy Spirit), the one who is now holding back the Man of Sin (the Antichrist), he cannot be revealed or loosed on the earth. Until we are in heaven and Jesus receives the scroll and looses the first seal, the Antichrist cannot come forth on the earth (Rev. 6:1-2). The white horse and the man with a bow was given a crown and went about conquering and to conquer. This is the revealing and loosing of the Antichrist and the beginning of the wrath of God. Satan doesn't control any events in the tribulation period other than what God allows him to do. All twenty-one judgments poured out upon the earth will be by God's authority and totally controlled by him. Man has rebelled against God and will pay the price for his disobedience. God jerks Satan's chain, and he does exactly what God wants him to do when he wants him to do it. Satan never had a chance of ever winning this war with God; he will face his final judgment with the Lord when he will be cast into the lake of fire forever (Rev. 20:10). He was never any match against our God, nor is man, but they have chosen their judgment, and they too will forever be separated from the one who truly loved them (John 3:36, Matt. 25:46). All the way, throughout the Word of God, he has told us every step of the past and present conditions and what the future holds for his children (John 16:13). The Holy Spirit has revealed these things to us if we will but study and receive his truth.

God is not trying to keep us in darkness about anything he says because we are children of light. We are not in darkness to be caught unaware (1 Thess. 5:4-5).

The eighth revelation of why we are in heaven before the tribulation is in the book of Daniel (Dan. 7:13). It states that the Son of Man, "coming with the clouds of heaven," comes to the ancient of days, and they bring us near before him. The clouds of heaven represent us, the saints. We are with him in heaven when he receives dominion and glory and a kingdom (Rev. 5:1-14). We have already described this. But what

I want to show you is that we must be in heaven to come back with him at the end of the seven years of tribulation in Revelation 19:11-14. Now take a look at what Jude 1:14-15 says. "Now Enoch prophesied, 'Behold the Lord comes with ten thousands of his saints to execute judgment on all ungodly sinners.'" This will happen when Jesus comes back to earth with us to judge the nations (Matt. 25:32-46) after this separation of sheep and goats. The sheep nations and all that enter the millennium reign, or one thousand years of peace, will all be saved, and a time of prosperity will begin. According to Isaiah 65:17-25, Jerusalem will become a joy, not a burden. Longevity will take place; people will begin to live a thousand years again like the time of old in the Garden of Eden. If an infant dies at one hundred years old, he will still be a child. Sickness will be a thing of old. Houses and food will be plentiful. Children will be born as blessings. The wolf and lamb shall eat together; the lion shall eat straw and lie down with the ox. The curse of the earth will be gone and there will be no more wars —just wonderful peace and plenty. Prayers will be answered before we are through praying.

The goat nations, or those who did not help the Jewish people and believers during the tribulation period, will be cast into the abode of the dead called Hades where the rest of the unrighteous or sinners are. They will wait for judgment at the White Throne Judgment of God. When all the unrighteous will be raised at the end of the one-thousand-year rule of peace of Christ (Rev. 20:11-15), the books will be opened, and every one of them will be given their opportunity to appear before God. Let me just say that God judges righteously (Rev. 19:11). No one will be cast into hell who doesn't deserve it. If God sends witness after witness to a sinner, and he refuses his mercy and forgiveness and chooses his own way and will not believe but wants nothing to do with God, there is nothing else God can do but judge him. There are only two places to live in eternity—in heaven with him or in hell separated from him. God wishes none should perish but that all of us come to the knowledge of the truth of Jesus, the Son of God, and his work of the cross (2 Pet. 3:9) and repent and be saved.

I hope you will pray and know that God will take us out of this world before he brings his judgments on this world. These eight reasons we must be in heaven before they are loosed, I pray, will bring comfort to your heart and let you rest in peace that God, our Father, loves you with all his heart, and he will not let any harm come to you. He is in control of every move that is made in our lives. He had the apostle Paul tell us in 2 Thessalonians 2:1-2 that we should not be shaken in mind or troubled by spirit or word about our gathering together in him (verse 1) as if that day of Christ had come.

It has not come yet, and when it does, you will disappear from this earth before any of these things (the Antichrist or the tribulation period) can begin.

CHAPTER 5

REVIEW OF ALL THESE THINGS

In this closing chapter, let's review and look at the complete plan of God in its simplest form, from the beginning before Creation to the close of the White Throne Judgment, and see how all these pieces of the big picture fit together in God's total plan for mankind's future. All this ties in with Satan and man's judgments along with that of all fallen angels. These things have to take place for righteous order to be restored in God's kingdom.

But the *catching-away* of the church is not a surprise to those that know their Bible. There have been several raptures in the Bible, and I want you to look at some of them so that you understand God has already showed us how quickly he can take us from the earth but will not do it without first revealing to us the general time (John 16:13) through the Holy Spirit and the Word. He said in the last days he would pour out his spirit on all flesh. Your sons and daughters shall prophesy. Your young men shall see visions; your old men shall dream dreams (Acts 2:17). At twenty-three years of age, this is what God did for me when he took me in the future in a vision to show me the reality of the rapture of the saints. I now have shared this vision with all that read this book.

God doesn't give us something to keep to ourselves but to give away—to enlarge and grow in faith. He loves his children and wants to comfort us in a world gone mad, eaten up with filth and evil all around us; we see the falling away from God, his Word and commandments replaced with humanism and those that think they are gods within themselves. Every cult is lifted up and promoted. If the name of Christ is mentioned in schools, the students are sent home or fail their grades and are treated like low-class citizens and inferior to the all-knowing and politically correct teachers and professors of our colleges (most of them) were founded on Christian principles and Christian values. God calls them false teachers and false apostles (Titus 1:16, Rev. 2:2). Some don't even try to hide their hatred of Jesus. They are, at least, honest in their pronouncement of being atheists. They say they don't believe in any gods. But to make this statement, they have to believe there are no gods (their faith), which is a religion in itself. God says the fool says in his heart, "There is no God" (Ps. 14:1). This is what you wake up to every day now in this generation.

But God, our father, does not want you to lose faith. He has a plan; it's already laid out in his Word. He has given the body good Bible teachers and pastors that are relaying the good news of salvation and truth, visions to young men, dreams to older men and women to share and to let you know God knows every hair on your head, every prayer you have ever prayed, every move you make, and every thought in your mind. He knew you before you were ever formed in your mother's belly (Jer. 1:8). He knows your past and your future; the plans that he has for you are good plans, not evil (Jer. 29:11). God has told us to look up because he is coming back for us (Luke 21:28). These signs that Jesus spoke of are now happening right before our eyes. Get ready to leave this earth. He is coming back for us. We are going to heaven, to the Father's house.

Well! You think I forgot about sharing the different scriptures that talk about those that have been raptured before us, so let's take a look at some of them.

The first rapture or catching up of a saint is found in Genesis 5:21-24. Enoch walked with God for over three hundred years. He pleased the Lord so much that God just took him up to heaven. The first sixty-five years of his life were spent in the world without walking with God, just like some of our lives. For thirty-three and a half years of my life, I was "unsaved," living with the devil in charge of it, thinking that every decision and every thought in my head were the ones I conceived on my own, not knowing anything about the war going on around me in the spiritual realm (Eph. 6:12) between God and the fallen angels (demons), a battle for the eternal souls of mankind. I was a slave to Satan (Rom. 6:16-18), a slave of sin on my way to death (hell), but thanks be to God for setting me free of sin through Christ and making me a slave of righteousness. Satan no longer has a hold on a man or woman of righteousness that has turned their life over to him.

Enoch became that man who walked with God and honored him in every way. Abraham might have been the friend of God, but Enoch pleased God so much God took him into heaven to be with him to be in his presence. He just disappeared from the earth. I'm sure all his friends and relatives looked for him, trying to discover what happened to him, but he was not to be found on planet Earth any longer. He was raptured from the generations and times of troubles coming upon the nations. Did you notice that Enoch begot Methuselah after, who walked with God three hundred years, then God took him? Methuselah lived to be 969 years of age, 669 years after his father was taken into heaven. Methuselah's name means that after death, the floods would come. Noah and his sons and their wives would be the only ones (eight people) that would make it out alive after the flood. The world fell into sin and evil during this time after Enoch's rapture. It was so evil by the time of Noah that God said that every intent of their thoughts was only evil. Continually he was sorry that he had made man on the earth and was grieved in his heart (Gen. 6:5-6).

Only one man found grace in God's eyes—Noah and his family. They made it through this time of tribulation, but tens of thousands died, and all of them were without God's grace. Listen carefully to what I am about to reveal. Enoch's case was a type of rapture of the church. He was taken out of this world just like the Body of Christ will be taken out of this earth (Rev. 3:10) just before the tribulation period of our generation begins (1 Cor. 15:50-52, 1 Thess. 4:13-18). We will be taken into heaven to be with the physical Jesus, the bridegroom, where we will stay for seven years. God will go back to dealing with the physical bloodline of Noah. The Jewish people that came from Noah to, eventually, Abraham, to the twelve tribes out of Jacob, to the people today (2013) gathered in Israel just like Noah. God will not take them out of this world, but he will keep them during the seven years of tribulation that will come upon the earth with the signing of a peace treaty with the Antichrist. The ark of safety in these days will be coming to the Messiah. The one they rejected 2000 years ago. God starts the ark by immediately sealing 144,000 Jewish evangelists at the very beginning of it (Rev. 7:1-4). They will receive the revelation of Jesus and be born again, I believe just like Saul, or Paul, did in Acts 9:3-6.

The second catching-away or rapture is found in 2 Kings 2:1-11. Elijah was about to be taken up into heaven by a chariot of fire. He had told his prophets at Bethel that God was coming to take him to heaven, so they were already aware that God was going to catch him away or rapture him (2 Kings 2:3). What amazes me is the Bible has told us in several solid scriptures (1 Cor. 15:50-52, 1 Thess. 4:13-16, Rev. 4:1, Rev. 3:10) that the Lord is coming back for us also. He will catch us up in the air, and we too will go into heaven to be with the Lord. There are those that believe in the catching-away of Enoch and Elijah, but when it comes to the teachings of the Rapture of the Church before tribulation, they have a hard time believing God would take us out of this earth to escape all these judgments.

Enoch was an example of the church taken out of the world before the flood or tribulation of his time. Elijah is also a type of pretribulation rapture with him taken into heaven, and Elisha, a type of the Jewish people left to walk through the trials on earth. God does not surprise us with any secret rapture, as some teach, but he reveals fully to his servants exactly what he is about to do (Deut. 29:29, 1 Cor. 2:10). For those who do not know God's Word or who do not study the Word for themselves but just hear some preaching doctrine on a subject, never checking out the scriptures for themselves, they will never receive true revelation from the Holy Spirit (John 8:31-32). You must stay in the Word and seek until you find what God wants to show you. Then the Holy Spirit in you will reveal these truths to you to know and no longer be tossed to and fro by every doctrine (Eph. 4:11-16).

The Lord has given the five-fold ministry to help you grow up, but it will take the Holy Spirit to enlighten you in his Word and bring you to all truth (John 14:26). God has given all of us a command from the apostle Paul to renew our minds and not to be conformed to this world so that we may prove (know) what is the good, acceptable, and perfect *will* of (Rom. 12:2) God. This cannot happen by going to church three times a week and just praying. It takes hours of reading the Bible and meditating on scripture promises, getting it down in your spirit, building faith to use in this world (Rom. 10:12). Keep reading and hearing until you can instantly bring it to memory when you need it in a time of trial. Begin to employ it in every situation you find yourself in. Speak against and resist the wiles of the devil (1 Pet. 5:8-9). God wants us to grow up and become strong men or women of God to overcome all problems in this world.

Let's move on to the third time God shows us total control over the body and the spirit. There are three times the spirit has left the body after death and God has called their spirits back into their bodies. In Luke 7:11-14, in the city of Nain, a widow's son had just died. His body was taken out to be buried when Jesus had compassion for the widow and called his spirit back into his body, and he sat up alive. The second time was in Matthew 8:23-26 when he came to Jairus's house and raised up his twelve-year-old daughter who had died (Luke 8:41-56). He sent out all the unbelievers that were mocking him because she had died. He told the mother and father not to weep, that she was not dead but just sleeping. He told her to arise. Her spirit came back into her body, and Jesus told her to eat something and charged her parents to tell no one. The third time is found in John 11:1-44 where Lazarus got sick and died. Jesus waited four days after his death before going to Bethany to raise him from the dead in Luke 16:19-31.

God gives us a look into life after death when the spirit, before Jesus's crucifixion, went to the abode of the dead. The righteous souls went to upper paradise, and the unrighteous went to lower Hades to wait for judgment. I want you to take a good look into the spirit realm to understand that it is no harder for God to call your spirit back into your body than it is for him to take you and your physical body out of this world into heaven. This is the reverse of what God did when he took Enoch and Elijah home to be with him. After Jesus's resurrection, he took from upper Hades or paradise all the people who were in covenant with him—back to heaven from Adam to his resurrection. Now when a person dies in Christ, we immediately enter his presence in heaven (2 Cor. 5:8).

God has total control of the rapture of his body or church. When the trumpet sounds, our bodies instantly die faster than you can blink your eye (1 Cor. 15:50-51). He *wraps* a new incorruptible body around our born-again godly spirit just like the one that Jesus has (1 John 3:1-2). This brings us to the fourth example of how God will catch away the church. When Christ was raised from the dead, the stone was rolled back from his tomb, and Mary could not find him because the angels then told her he was not there but he had risen. Mary did not physically see his transformation because it was invisible to the world, but later, Jesus appeared to her in his glorified body (Matt. 28:1-10).

The same thing is going to happen when the Rapture of the Church takes place. We will disappear to the world when Jesus comes back in the air to receive us (1 Thess. 4:13-16). Later, at the end of the tribulation period, we will all come back with him (Rev. 19:11-17), and then the world will see him physically (Rev. 11:19, Rev. 1:7) as the King of Kings and the Lord of Lords. But this time, his feet will touch the Mt. of Olives. It will split north and south; there will also be a great earthquake (Zech. 14:3-5). In verse 6, it also says that the Lord comes back with all his saints. That means we will be with him.

The fifth rapture of the Bible is the "catching-away of the saints" (1 Cor. 15:50-51). This should not surprise anyone that understands God's Word. Jesus will come again to take us home to be with him (Acts 1:11). The same way he was taken up into the clouds will be the same way he descends in the clouds to receive us to himself. In my vision of the rapture in 1973, this same Jesus was descending to meet me in the air as I rose to meet him. I could end right here on our discussions of the different ways that God has taken his people from the earth to heaven, and I believe you now have a better understanding of why and how he will do this. But the truth is, after the church has been raptured, there are still more catching-aways in the future.

In the book of Revelation, we see where a sixth group of people will be taken up to heaven after three and a half to four years into the tribulation period. In Revelation 7:1-8, we see where God goes back to dealing with the nation of Israel by sealing 144,000 Jewish evangelists. These will be the end-time preachers that will win tens of thousands of people for Christ out of every nation—tribes, people, and tongues (Rev. 7:9-10). They will all be tribulation saints. The greatest revival of all time will take place during the last seven years of mankind's rule. The 144,000 will preach the first three and a half to four years of tribulation, then God will send his two witnesses with all power to preach and battle Satan and the Antichrist until the last four days of the tribulation period. After the 144,000 ministry is finished, they will be raptured into heaven to be with Jesus and the saints (Rev. 14:1-5). Verse 3 says they are before the throne and were redeemed from the earth. This rapture also brings to heaven all those that were saved during their ministry (Rev. 7:9). These are the ones who come out of the great tribulation, clothed in white robes, with palm branches in the hands, which represent the Jewish revival that takes place in the world.

Revelation 1:7

The seventh and final rapture will take place at the last day of the tribulation period when the two witnesses will finally be killed by the Antichrist. The world will be so happy that they have been killed they will give gifts to each other around the world, celebrating the victory of the Antichrist, rejoicing that these troublemakers have finally been killed. They will leave their bodies lying in the street for the whole world to see. Cameras around the world will be turned on them to watch their bodies rot in the street. But are they in for a big surprise (Rev. 11:3-12). On the very last day of the fulfillment of all the days allotted for the tribulation period (2,520 days), from the beginning of the signing of a seven-year peace treaty to this day, the last day, all of a sudden, the clouds will roll back, and a voice from heaven will be saying, "Come up here." The spirit of these two witnesses will come back into their bodies, and they will rise up in the air and ascend into heaven. Every TV network in the world will broadcast this around the world. Every eye shall see this happen. The world will get to behold Jesus with his saints come from heaven and back to this world on white horses, ready to battle all his enemies that are gathered against him (Rev. 19:11-14) and us.

Fear will fall upon the whole world as they see Christ and his saints coming back to earth. Christ will now have taken back dominion over the earth, and the kingdom of the world will now became the kingdom of God and his Christ (Rev. 11:15), the harvest of the earth. He will thrust in his sickle and gather the cluster of grapes that are fully ripe (Rev. 14:14-20) and throw them into the wineries (which represents the armies gathered at the Valley of Armageddon). The blood will run up to the horse's bridle for 14 miles wide and 180 miles long. This is the price the world pays when God no longer has a place in their lives. Most of the people that die during these seven years will miss God and go into judgment (Rev. 6:8). They will make the choice to take the mark of the Beast or want to control the world. Their pride in themselves will want power—control over others and possession of their wealth—in the end, their own greed will destroy them. Let's go back for just a second and talk about the two witnesses. There are those in the body who believe these two witnesses are Enoch and Elijah, who have not yet had to die in the flesh. So God takes them from the heaven they were raptured to back to the earth in the last three and a half years to combat the Antichrist and Satan. God will allow the Antichrist to overcome them on the very last four days of tribulation just before he comes back with his saints to judge the nation of the earth.

This could be a real possibility since in Malachi 4:5, the Lord says that before the coming of the great and dreadful day of the Lord, he would send Elijah the prophet. Enoch also did not experience physical death when God took him into heaven, so many believe both of these men will experience physical death at the end of the tribulation period. The truth is, no one really knows for sure exactly what or who these witnesses will be. We do know that these men will have the same anointing and power that God gave Elijah in the Old Testament. God will be able to raise in our generation two men who can and will carry out his will with faithfulness unto death. The reason I believe this is because Jesus, in Matthew 11:14, made a statement about John the Baptist and him being more than just a prophet. He said that among those born of a woman, there has not risen one greater than him. And if we were willing to receive it, he is Elijah! Who is to come—what he was saying—is the same spirit that was upon Elijah was also upon John the Baptist. "Because it's not by might nor by power but by my spirit," says the Lord (Zech. 4:6). God can place and put his spirit of power upon whoever he chooses, but whatever God chooses, his will shall be done on earth as it is in heaven (Matt. 6:10).

As you can see, through revealing to the church seven different times, God has raptured or caught-away his people—those from the past, Enoch and Elijah; Jesus, two thousand years ago; and now his body, the church, will be taken out of this world. It will happen shortly before the tribulation period can begin. Later we see the 144,000 Jewish evangelists and the tribulation saints caught up to heaven to be with Jesus and his bride. And finally these two witnesses, right at the end of tribulation, to be raptured to heaven to be with all of us as Jesus comes back to earth to take control of all kingdoms and judge and rule the earth for his one thousand years of peace.

CONCLUSION

The testimony of my vision of the rapture in 1973 is true and as clear to me today as it was then. I still see the clouds rolling back and the angels coming forth to blow their trumpets—the wonderful sound that comes forth to call God's children home, gravity having to turn loose of all that belongs to Christ, rising out of that vehicle, looking up, and seeing the Savior with his hands outstretched, descending on those golden rays of sunlight to meet me in the air.

God will give us a brand-new body on that day, a body that will no longer hurt or have pain, one that will still enjoy all the wonderful feelings of joy and happiness. All our senses will be heightened. Colors will be extremely clear and more vivid. You will be known even as our Lord is known. You will know and recognize people like Abraham, Sarah, and Jacob even though you have not met them before. Your mind will be opened by the spirit of the Lord to operate at full capabilities.

I believe we will be able to move at the speed of thought. Faster than you can think where to go, you will be there.

Heaven will not be a boring place where everyone plays harps all day. (We will not sit on clouds all day singing!) God has greater plans for his children, the same way you as a father or mother want to share with your child the things you have learned in life. If the father is a welder or electrician and has a son, he can't wait to teach him his trade, or a mother teaches her daughter how to bake cookies and cook a meal. Picture our Father, God, who has created billions of beings, from angels to seraphims, or four living creatures with six wings (Rev. 4:8), also billions of other worlds and kingdoms that your mind cannot even imagine (1 Cor. 2:9). It has not yet even entered into your mind the vastness of God's kingdom. Picture the sands of a seashore, then pick up one grain of sand—it represents earth, and all the other mountains of sand around you represent God's kingdom. Even after a zillion times zillion years, you will not yet have graduated kindergarten in all the things God your father wants to show you. No, my friends, heaven will not be boring. Eternity will be the most exciting place you could ever be.

Jesus has given to his bride a great gift, not only salvation of our souls but he declared that we would also be "joint heirs" with him in his kingdom (Rom. 8:16-17). But in this life, we must also be willing to suffer with him, a small price to pay when we consider everything he has done for us. He said that many would miss the narrow road of salvation to heaven and follow the broad road of destruction. The narrow way is only through his blood and cross that we can be saved. Jesus said, "I am the way, the life and truth." No one comes to the father (John 14:6) except by him, by being in Christ; there is no other way to go to heaven. No other religion or belief will get you there. There are not many ways to God, *only one*. Any other will guarantee that you go to hell. You will be on the broad road of hell's judgment. Many claim to know God the Father but deny the Son (1 John 2:21-23). There is no life in them if they do not die in Christ where Christ himself paid for their deaths. They will have to die in their flesh and pay for their own sins. The Bible says that the wage of sin is death (Rom. 6:23), but the gift of God is eternal life in Christ Jesus our Lord. Make your choice—die in yourself and sin or make Jesus the Lord of your life by repeating this prayer with me. If you have not done so, now is your day of salvation.

Pray this prayer with me to be saved: "Lord God, please forgive me of my sins. I believe in my heart that you sent your son, Jesus, to this earth to die for me. Through his death, burial, and resurrection, I can have new life in him. Lord Jesus, forgive me of my sins, and come into my heart. Be my savior, my king, and my lord. From this moment forward, I will serve only you. Thank you for saving me—in *your name* I pray. Amen."

If you have prayed this prayer in faith, believing the Lord has accepted you as his child and forgives you of all your sins, he will want you to get into a Bible-believing church in your area, and he will begin to teach you his Word and lead you into all truth. He will direct your life into holiness and make sure you bear fruit for the kingdom of God. Don't worry about what kind of ministry he has for you. As you grow in his Word, it will become clearer and more pronounced as time passes. He may not call you to be a pulpit minister, but he will call you to be a minister, maybe for help or giving. It could be helping in the church to fulfill a need. Whatever it will be, it is just as important as a Billy Graham preaching to thousands. The person who waters a ministry will share equally in rewards as the person who sows (1 Cor. 3:6-8). God has a plan for your life right now, and he means it for good (John 28:11). Many voices will be raised to try to discourage you, but listen to the voice of the Good Shepherd in you—he will direct your path, and you will not fail (John 10:3-4).

The Christian walk will not be easy. People will call you closed-minded, a bigot, someone who will not tolerate other religious ways to heaven. You think you are right and everyone else is wrong. Your belief is the only one. You will have to stand strong in your faith for Christ because they are "right"—Jesus is the only way. There is no other religion; it's either heaven with him or hell without. In Luke 8, it talks about the world as it falls on four different types of soil. You have to determine which "soil" you are. In verse 12, the Word fell by

(1) the *wayside*—they heard the Word, but Satan immediately came and took it from their hearts lest they be saved; and on
(2) stony ground or rock the Word fell. They received it with joy for a while but it had no root, so when temptation came, they fell away.
(3) thorny ground; when they heard the Word, they were choked with the cares of this world and produced no fruit to maturity.
(4) was when the Word fell upon an open or noble good heart. They kept it and bore fruit with patience.

Out of these four different soils, the Lord shows us that three of them failed. Only one soil (the good soil) showed us the saved person, producing the fruit of the kingdom.

The first—Satan stole the Word before he could be saved.

The second had *no root* in him. Jesus is the root—without him, there is no life (John 15:5). He is the true view.

The third let the world and its cares deceive him, choke out his life of the Word, and the world was more important than God.

But the fourth soil—the people listened about Christ, opened their hearts to believe and receive, then they went out and began to live their lives for him and produce fruit.

How you believe the Word and its Christ will determine your destiny. Live for Christ, and he will bring you through the cares of this world, and even though you and I walk through the valley of the shadow of death, we shall live with him for eternity (Ps. 23:4). I will fear no evil for you are with me. Trust the Lord, and he will bring you through.

I hope my vision of the Rapture of the Church has opened your heart to understand how much God loves you and how he wants all of us to know he is coming back for his bride and he will not allow any *tribulation hurt* to come to her.

When I was praying to the Lord about this book and why he had me wait thirty years from the time of my new birth (March 27, 1983) to today in 2013 to write it (the vision he gave me of the rapture), he asked me a question! How old was his son, Jesus, when he began his ministry? I thought about it for a minute and replied that he was thirty years of age before entering and did his first miracle at the wedding in Cana (John 2:11), turning water into wine. The Lord spoke to my heart that even his son had to be trained up for thirty years, taught by his spirit before fulfilling his ministry on earth.

I too for thirty years had to walk and learn by the Holy Spirit those things in his Word that I would write today. The Lord wanted his people to hear his voice clearly from his Word—the message of him catching them away to be with him to comfort them and tell them not to fear, that before the terrible day of his wrath on earth, they would be safely in his hands.

Before the Antichrist or seal judgments or before any trumpets could sound or be loosed, we would be singing in heaven before his throne (Rev. 5:4:11). We are that sea of glass around the throne of God.

It's not my intention to offend any believers in Christ that may have a different view of this doctrine. We all have a choice to follow our teachers and their understanding of God's Word. There are many good teachers and preachers in the body of Christ that believe as sincerely as I do in what God has shown them.

This is what God has shown me to give to you in these last days. You will have to pray and ask the Holy Spirit to witness with your spirit if these words are true (Rom. 8:16). I couldn't write them in 1973 (I wasn't born-again). I could not write them in 1983 because I didn't have the Word of God in me (but I was born again!). After training for thirty years, I still only have a drop in the bucket of God's knowledge. Seventeen of those years were spent in education until I received my PsyD in scriptural psychology in the year 2000. If we live another fifty years, we will not stop learning and growing in the knowledge of the Lord. May God bless you in every step you take for him.

In Jesus's name,
Dr. Richard E. Weathers, PsyD

It is amazing how fast time goes by, it is now "<u>2023</u>" and a lot of things revealed in these pages that were for the <u>future</u> in 2013 are now becoming <u>present</u> in this age by the Holy Spirit.

The inflation in our country is rapidly destroying the economy and the dollar – The government has it at 6 to 7%, where it is actually closer to 18 to 20%. Food and gas prices are increasing faster than income. The national debt we talked about in 2013 – that it would be 22 trillion by 2020 was and now – is 31 trillion.

They are now developing a digital cryptocurrency that will control every transaction you make at the bank and stores (you) purchase goods or materials. This will be put in place from 2023 to 2025.

More and more taxes will be raised on all those that still have assets (like houses, businesses, and investments). You may not be aware of it – but they have already got control of your 401k and IRA investment accounts that are for your retirement. There are about 3 trillion dollars sitting in these hands-on.

It is not by accident that those now in authority in our government are trying to destroy our nation and our freedom of speech and take away our right to defend our families and ourselves. They are now doing this by executive orders of a president against our constitution. He has sworn to uphold the same constitution and protect it – to also protect our nation from outside invaders but instead has opened our southern borders to our enemies and criminals plus drug cartels that bring in drugs across the border to kill our children. The word tells us to (Rev. 16:11) they blasphemed God and still will not repent of their evil deeds – (Rev. 9:21) also, they will not repent of their murders or their sorceries, sexual immorality or their thefts. They have now voted in laws that break "<u>everyone</u>" of God's 10 Commandments.

Murder – Passing laws in 1973 so women can kill thus little babies in the womb called abortion (Psm 139:13-16) and (Jer 1:15).

Sorceries – "GK" Pharmacia where we get our word for medicines and drugs. Doctors have been turning people into druggies for a long time giving them pain pills and they come dependent on them – states are passing laws legalizing the use of marijuana.

Sexual Immorality – Voting in-laws to protect homosexual and lesbian marriage. They have laws pending trying to make it a crime if you speak out against this abominable sin (rom 1:18-32) (I Cor 6:9-12). Those that practice these sins will have their judgment in the "Lake of Fire" (Jude 1:7) I John 3:7-8.

Thefts – Our own government now has passed trillions of dollars in spending bills and has destroyed our ability to ever pay it back – our children in the future are now in debt to hundreds of thousands of dollars and debt they did not cause – the Democrats and Republicans have done this to us (we today owe 32 trillion dollars and the world together owes 300 trillion dollars of debt.

This all sounds terrible and it is but remembers God is in control and what is happening right now is what he told us would take place just before he comes.

All the signs pointing to Christ coming back to earth are now playing themselves out right before our eyes. Jesus asked us to believe in his work on the cross, that through his death, buried, and resurrection we through "Faith" would be saved (Rom 10:9-10).

We are but a moment away from Jesus coming for his church the Lord has waited until now to put this book in your hands – it is not by accident that you have it today.

The Lord has called forth a publisher (The Ewings Publishing House) to bring this book to many nations to help open their eyes to what is happening in our world today and what is about to happen after we are gone from this earth in the rapture or catching away of his body.

Many are going to be confused about what is going on. We believe this book will help those that are left understand what will happen after their loved ones are gone or disappear.

I look at what we have shared on these pages is just now taking place.

In Matt 24:5 – The Lord talks about deceivers, pestilences, and earthquakes in different places in 2020 we have now been through a virus called Covid 19. A plaque that has shut down an entire world – there was only one other time the world was shut down and that was when God flooded the earth and drown the known world of Noah: time (Gen 6:1).

This plaque of Covid is just a taste of what is going to happen during the tribulation period. We watched a president through executive action (like a dictator) try to control people to wear a mask or take a covid shot against the constitution and the will of the people to choose themselves. Even to the control of dismissing thousands of workers from their jobs (if they didn't take it) or giving a dishonorable discharge to our military men and woman.

Businesses like Walmart in California would not let people in to buy merchandise or food unless they could present a certification showing they had taken the "shot".

This my friend is a forerunner in (Rev 13:16-17). People will not be able to buy or sell during this time. God is showing us today through these examples what is about to happen in the future.

Earthquakes and floods are taking place today around the world. Volcanos are about to erupt and destroy a lot of cities and people.

Famines are now destroying our food production and our rivers are drying up and fires are burning down our trees and mud slides are everywhere.

I write these warnings not to frighten anyone but to remind you what Jesus said in (Luke 21:25-28) (To look up because our redemption is drawing wear.)

We are about to be raptured and go to the fathers' house (John 14:1-6).

We will not go through any of God's wrath (Rev 3:10) but spend seven years in heaven with Christ before coming back to earth (after the tribulation period) to rule with Christ for a thousand years on earth (I Thes 4:18) comfort one another with these words.

It has now been about 50 years (1973-2023) since Jesus took me into the future and let me experience the rapture or catching away (I Thes 4:17) of his body or church.

The year 50 represents in the bible a Jubilee year. A time that God resets the world and releases it from its debts.

2023 is going to be an exciting year for the Christians God is about to release us from this earth. We will have our trials and tribulation but with an expectant heart, we know that the Lord is coming soon and we are looking up to Christ's return.

Keep praying and remember God has you in the palm of his hand and no one can pluck you out of his hand (John 10:28).

Love in Christ
Dr. Richard Weathers, PsyD.

P.S.
Please share this book with a loved one and pray they will receive it with an open heart.

REFERENCES

Time Is Up
Raptured

1) *From Eternity to Heaven*, pages 107-112
   French Viola—The Jewish Wedding

2) All scriptures from the New King James Version for this book

God's Psychology

1) *Psychology: An Introduction*
   7th edition, Benjamin B. Lahey
   Sigmund Freud, pages 12-13, 397-399, 468-470

2) All scriptures from the New King James Version

INDEX

A

abomination, 46, 58-59
Abraham, 32, 34-35, 42, 75-76, 81
Adam, 30, 32, 41, 43, 78
altar, 22, 34, 42, 46
angels, 17, 26, 31-32, 35, 41, 59, 78, 81
    fallen, 32, 74-75
Antichrist, 17, 24, 28-29, 36-37, 40, 48-50, 56, 58, 64-68, 70-71, 73, 76, 79-80, 84
apostasy, 37, 71
Armageddon, 56, 66, 68, 79
armies, 40-41, 45, 56-57, 67-68, 79
army, two-hundred-million-man, 40, 56, 63-65

B

Babylonian Empire, 44
Beast, the, 27, 48, 50, 80
mark of, 27, 80
belief, 26, 47, 55, 82-83
believers, 45, 57, 69, 72, 84
born-again, 35, 37
Berlin Wall, 63
Bible, 18, 29, 34-35, 40, 46-47, 50, 53-55, 58, 60, 63-64, 66-68, 71, 74, 76-78, 82
bigot, 53, 60, 83
Blue Springs, 16, 18, 23
body, physical, 45, 78
Body of Christ, 70, 76
bondages, 24-25, 42
Branson, 18
bridal chamber, 38-39
bride, 25, 27-28, 33, 35-39, 44, 68-69, 80, 82-83
bridegroom, 38-39, 76

C

Calvary, 16, 33, 71
Canaan, 42
China, 45, 53, 57, 63-64, 67
Christianity, 26
Christians, 26, 28, 47, 64-65, 69
Christian values, 75
church, 11, 15, 17, 19, 23-27, 33, 35-38, 40, 42-44, 46-47, 58, 61, 64-65, 68-71, 74, 76-78, 80, 82-83

clouds, 17-18, 26, 35, 48, 72, 78-79, 81
Cold War, 63
Columbia, 20
computers, 28, 50
condemnation, 24, 60
congregation, 20-22
conscience, 41
constitution, 49, 55, 60-61
covenant, 32, 34, 37, 43, 58, 65, 67, 78
cults, 34, 43, 74
currency, 62

D

darkness, 15, 21-22, 32, 49, 72
Dead Sea, 40
death, 15-16, 22, 24, 26, 29-30, 32, 41-42, 46-47, 55, 58, 75-77, 80, 82
deceivers, 34, 47-48
deliverance, 15, 27, 31, 69
demons, 22, 32, 75
devil, 46-47, 60, 67, 70, 75, 77
disappearance, 37, 64-65
disobedience, 33, 68, 71
dispensation, 41-42, 70
doctrines, 23, 25, 35, 77, 84
dominion, 31-32, 41, 72, 79

E

earth, 15, 17, 21-23, 25-32, 34-37, 39-45, 48-50, 56-64, 67-82, 84
earthquakes, 29, 40, 65, 78
economy, 48-49, 54, 64
Elijah, 76-77, 80
Enoch, 72, 75-78, 80

eternity, 22, 27, 58, 68-69, 72, 82-83, 85
Eve, 30, 41
evil, 24, 32, 41, 59-60, 74-76, 83

F

faith, 16, 24, 26, 33, 47-48, 55-56, 58, 65, 74-75, 82-83
false Christs, 46, 48
father's house, 27, 37-39, 44, 68, 75
fear, spirit of, 11, 24-25, 27, 59, 65, 69, 79, 83-84
flesh, 37, 39, 46-47, 55, 74, 80, 82
floods, 29, 32, 41, 65, 76-77
freedom, 54

G

Garden of Eden, 31, 41, 72
generations, 23, 29, 34-35, 44-46, 48, 50, 55-57, 60-62, 65, 75-76, 80
Gentile, 34, 43, 64
gifts, 38, 79, 82
glory, earthly, 47
goat nations, 72
God, 9, 11, 15-18, 20, 22-37, 39-50, 55-61, 64-85
  wrath of, 29, 35, 37, 69, 71
Gomorrah, 59
government, 48-49, 53-55, 64-65, 67
  one-world, 27, 48, 54, 61
groom, 37

H

Hades, 43, 72, 78
Ham, 41

heaven, 16-18, 23-24, 26, 30-32, 34-35, 37, 39, 41-49, 55, 57-58, 61, 65, 68-73, 75-85
Heaven's Gate, 47
hell, 26, 34, 39, 43, 47, 49, 53, 72-73, 75, 82-83
holiness, 24, 34, 82
homosexuality, 26, 48, 59
humanity, 39-40, 46

I

India, 45, 56, 64
Iowa, 7
Iran, 45, 56-58, 66
Iraq, 56, 58
Israel, 29, 33-36, 39, 42, 44-46, 56-58, 64-67, 76, 79

J

Jerusalem, 33-34, 36, 40, 45, 57, 72
Jesus Christ, 16, 22, 24, 26-29, 32-39, 42-44, 46-49, 55-56, 58-60, 65, 68-73, 75-80, 82-84
   blood of, 26, 33, 43
Jewish evangelists, 70, 76, 79-80
Jewish marriage, 37-39
Jews, 33-34, 36, 40, 42-45, 57
Jezereel, 40, 65, 67
judgment, 23, 26, 32-33, 36, 43, 46, 55-56, 60, 69, 71-74, 76, 78, 80
   final, 26, 71
Justin, 9, 19-20

K

Kansas City, 7, 16, 18
Kay, 9, 18-20, 23
kingdom of God, 16, 33, 60, 69-70, 79, 82

L

language, 41-42
laws, 16, 33, 42, 48-49, 55, 59-60
Lazarus, 34, 77
leaders, 49, 55-56, 58, 60, 62, 65-67
life, eternal, 16, 26, 82
Lord, 9, 11, 19-20, 22-25, 27-28, 34, 37-40, 42, 44, 46, 50, 59, 61-62, 64, 68-72, 75-78, 80-84
Lot, 59
love, 11, 16, 20-23, 25-27, 39, 46, 48, 60, 68-69
Lucifer, 31

M

Magog, 56, 66
mankind, 24, 30-31, 35, 37, 41-43, 45, 56, 74-75
marking system, 50, 53-54, 58, 67
marriage, 9, 19, 37-39
marriage supper, 38-39
Mary, 78
Mediterranean, 40
Medo-Persian Empire, 42
Messiah, 33-34, 36, 40, 47, 64, 70, 76
Middle East, 56-57, 66-67
military, 62, 65-66
military power, 63
ministry, 8-9, 23, 34, 47, 79, 82, 84
miracles, 35, 48
Missouri, 7-8, 16, 18-20, 23
money, 19, 49, 54, 62-63
Moses, 42
mountains, 17, 26, 40, 57, 66, 81
Muslims, 56-57

N

national ID card, 54
nationalities, 27
national leaders, 47
nations, 27-29, 32-35, 40, 42, 44-46, 49, 53-57, 59-60, 62-68, 72, 76, 79-80
Nimrod, 41
Noah, 32, 41, 76
nuclear warfare, 45

O

oceans, 30-31
oil, 38, 57, 66
Old Testament, 28, 33, 37, 39, 43, 80
Olive Branch Baptist Church, 23

P

pain, 20-21, 81
pastor, 8, 19-20, 75
peace, 25-27, 35-36, 39-41, 43, 45, 55, 63, 66-68, 72-73, 80
peace treaty, seven-year, 29, 36, 58, 66, 79
perversion, sin of, 59-60
plan of salvation, 15, 25, 32
power, 17, 27, 29, 36, 41, 45-46, 48-49, 62-64, 66-67, 69-71, 79-80
prayer, 28, 55, 58-60, 72, 75, 82
preachers, 24, 46-48, 55, 60, 70, 84
presidents, 49, 55-56, 59-60, 63, 66
pride, 16, 22, 31, 34, 80
privacy, 53
promised land, 42
prophecy, 28-29, 44, 48, 56-57, 61-62, 64
prophets, 43, 76, 80
  false, 34, 40, 48-49, 56, 67-68
proposal, 37

R

rapture, pretribulation, 77
Rapture of the Church, the, 33, 36, 43, 64-65, 68, 76, 78, 83
religions, 16, 26, 43, 55, 58, 75, 82-83
religious system, one-world, 48
religious works, 24, 33-34
righteousness, 16, 26, 33, 75
Roe v. Wade, 55
Roman Empire, 29, 34, 36, 64, 66
Russia, 45, 56-58, 63-64, 66

S

saints, 28-29, 37-40, 48, 65, 68, 70, 72, 74-75, 78-80
salvation, 15-16, 25-27, 29, 31-34, 37, 40, 43, 68-69, 75, 82
Satan, 25-26, 28, 31-32, 40, 46-47, 49, 67-68, 70-71, 74-75, 80, 83
schools, 55, 60, 74
scriptures, 23, 28-29, 35, 40, 44, 47, 54, 61, 68-69, 75, 77, 85
Seal Judgments, 24-25, 84
Sedalia, 7, 18-19, 23
servants, 40-41, 77
service, 7, 19-20, 22
sex, 55, 59-60
sheep, 53-54, 72
sheep nations, 45, 58, 72

signs, 29, 44-46, 48, 50, 56-57, 59, 61, 65-66, 75
sinners, 22, 46, 60, 72
slaves, 34, 42, 66, 75
Sodom, 59
soil, 83
soul, 21-22, 25-27, 32, 34, 36, 39, 53, 58, 75, 77, 82
spaceship, 47
spirit world, 41
Springfield, 7-8, 18-19
superpowers, 62-63, 66

T

taxes, 54, 64
temple, 23, 33-34, 36, 42, 45, 47, 58, 66-67, 71
Ten Commandments, 16, 42, 48, 55, 60
throne, 79, 84
Tonyja, 9, 19
treaties, 29, 57-58
Tree of Good and Evil, 32, 41
trial, 35, 37, 45, 69, 77
tribulation, 28, 33, 36-37, 39, 44-45, 50, 65-66, 68-72, 76-77, 79-80
tribulation saints, 70, 79-80
Trumpet Judgments, 25
trumpets, 17-18, 24, 26-27, 38, 70, 81, 84
truth, 24, 26, 30-31, 34, 36-37, 40, 46, 48, 54-55, 60, 65, 72-73, 75, 77-78, 80, 82

U

unbelievers, 27, 45, 49, 69, 77
United Nations (UN), 49, 54
United States of America, 25, 49, 56, 60, 62-66

V

Vial Judgment, 25
vision, 15-18, 23, 25-26, 28, 33, 39, 74-75, 78, 81, 83-84
voices, 27, 53, 79, 82-84

W

war, 17, 25, 29, 31, 40, 55, 64-68, 71, 75
weapons, 45-46, 62, 66
    nuclear, 45, 62-64
wedding guests, 38
White Throne Judgment, 72, 74
women, 24, 46, 55, 60, 75, 77
Word of God, 23, 28, 47, 70, 72, 84
world hunger, 67
world passport, 27-28
World War III, 57, 65-66
wrath, 23-27, 37, 40, 44, 68-71, 84

www.ingramcontent.com/pod-product-compliance
Lightning Source LLC
LaVergne TN
LVHW041615070526
838199LV00052B/3164